IVAN MEŠTROVIĆ

sculptor and patriot

IVAN

MEŠTROVIĆ

sculptor and patriot

LAURENCE SCHMECKEBIER

© 1959

SYRACUSE UNIVERSITY PRESS

Library of Congress Catalog Card Number: 59-7951

*This work has been published with the
assistance of a Ford Foundation grant.*

*Manufactured in the United States of America
by Photogravure & Color Company, New York, N. Y.*

Preface

To honor Ivan Meštrović during his seventy-fifth year, Syracuse University exhibited his recent work in January 1958. Here was demonstrated not only the continued vitality and extraordinary stature of this internationally famous sculptor, but,also the persistence of certain basic ideas of individual freedom and the rights of men which have made him both a political and artistic personality of significance for more than fifty years.

Fear of an ideological war has developed into a passion, and though the military campaigns may subside, the war of ideas persists. Artists have played a major role in the communication and conflict of ideas, and it is for this reason that the dual concept of patriot and sculptor seems especially important in reviewing the career of Ivan Meštrović.

Grateful thanks are given the artist, his family, and the many friends and patrons who have assisted so generously in the preparation of this book. Professor and Mrs. Meštrović have been most gracious in permitting the use of files, letters, records, and photographs. Their devoted cooperation has made the task of compilation a genuine pleasure. Their son, Dr. Matthew Meštrović, has given invaluable and scholarly assistance in checking dates, bibliography, and historical background. Mr. Mirko Zarić of the Embassy of Yugoslavia in Washington and Mr. Branko Novaković of the Yugoslav Information Office in New York have been exceptionally generous and cooperative in providing advice, information, and photographs. Most of the photographs of work in Yugoslavian museums were made possible through the assistance of Mr. Novaković.

Among the many others who gave invaluable assistance, I should like especially to thank Mr. Donald Anderson of the *Wisconsin State Journal*, Rev. Charles E. Sheedy, Dean of the College of Arts and Letters at Notre Dame University, Mr. R. E. Roesler of the Mayo Clinic, Rt. Rev. Msgr. Thomas I. Grady of the National Shrine of the Immaculate Conception,

Rev. Sebastian Loncar of the St. Jerome House of Studies, Washington, D.C., and Rt. Rev. Msgr. James T. Nolan of the Archbishop Stepinac High School, White Plains, N. Y., Dr. E. M. Levin of Syracuse.

A special word of appreciation is due Mr. Donald Bean, director of the Syracuse University Press, Mrs. Arpena Mesrobian, editor, and Mrs. Elizabeth Replogle, assistant, for their sympathetic enthusiasm. Page design and layout are by Robert Topor. Professor M. Peter Piening of the Syracuse University School of Art served as design consultant and is responsible for the design of cover and jacket. I am indebted to Dartmouth College for the privilege of using its excellent art library and to Miss Maude French, librarian, for her generous help. As always, the faithful assistance of Alexandra Schmeckebier deserves the author's deepest gratitude.

Acknowledgment is made for photographs reproduced as follows: Brooklyn Museum, Fig. 28; National Gallery of Canada (Ottawa), Fig. 36; Art Institute of Chicago, Fig. 39; Toronto Art Gallery, Fig. 40; Montreal Museum of Fine Arts, Fig. 172. Photographs of work in the Syracuse University collection were made by Oswald Werner.

The complete bibliography of notices and critical comments on the work of Ivan Meštrović runs into many thousands of items in a dozen different languages. Among the significant publications are: *Ivan Meštrović, a Monograph*, Milan Ćurčin, editor, London, 1919; *Ivan Meštrović*, by Ernest H. R. Collings, with an introduction by the artist, Zagreb, 1933; *Ivan Meštrović* by Harry Hilberry, Syracuse, 1948; *Gospa od Anđelâ: a Memorial Church of the Račić Family in Cavtat by Ivan Meštrović* by Josef Stryzgowski, Zagreb, 1937. Of the catalogues, the most important are: *The Meštrović Exhibition* (Brooklyn, 1924) by Christian Brinton; *Ivan Meštrović* (Paris Exposition, 1933) by Andre Dezarrois and R. Warnier; and *Katalog Galerije Ivana Meštrovića U Splitu* (Meštrović Gallery, Split, 1957). An interesting account of Meštrović in the early 1930's appears in *The Native's Return* by Louis Adamic, New York, 1934. The best description of the complex background and political relationship between Serbia and Croatia from Meštrović's point of view is given in P. D. Ostović's *The Truth about Yugoslavia*, with an introduction by Ivan Meštrović, New York, 1952. Meštrović's *Christmas Dialogue* was written in Croatian, translated into German by Dr. A. Licht, and published under the title, *Dennoch Will Ich Hoffen . . .*, Zurich, 1945. His study *Michelangelo* appeared in Croatian (*Nova Evropa*, November 1926), and *Dialogues with Michelangelo* was published in German (*Kunst ins Volk*, Vol. VIII, IX, Vienna, 1957-58). See *Yugoslav Sculpture of the Twentieth Century*, Oto Bihaji-Merin, Belgrade, 1955, for a general survey.

LAURENCE SCHMECKEBIER

Contents

Biographical Sketch

I

"Happy are those who live forever. They had a reason for being born." Thus Ivan Meštrović quoted the great Montenegrin poet Petar Petrović Njegoš in reference to the imprisonment of Aloysius Cardinal Stepinac, during an interview for the *Syracuse Herald-Journal* December 11, 1952.

Meštrović had known the heroic Croatian churchman for many years, believed him to be innocent of the political crimes of which he was accused, and deplored as did the entire civilized western world, his unjust imprisonment by the Communist masters of Yugoslavia. "Those who believe in immortal life," Meštrović went on, "are the more courageous. Stepinac and those like him believe that the true life cannot be shackled or destroyed. Therefore the struggle is between two unequal powers, one transitory and the other eternal. Those who hold the reins of power at the present moment should contemplate whose will be the ultimate victory."

The Ultimate Victory—the moment at hand or eternity, the things of the spirit or those of the flesh, the divine rights of the individual or the imposed standards of the mechanized masses—these are the issues of the twentieth century with which generations of statesmen, politicians, philosophers and artists have been deeply concerned. The lifelong achievement of Ivan Meštrović, the patriot as well as the sculptor, reveals one artist's attempt to point out the road to clarification of this most fundamental of human dilemmas.

It may well be that the artist does not need the critic, but he does need the historian. For, in the welter of shifting ideas, styles, standards, and purposes of what we call contemporary art, we sometimes lose sight of the really great men about us and fail to comprehend the genuine and significant ideas. The artists indeed are many, the great ones are few, and those whose motivation and artistic achievement reveal significant ideas are still fewer: witness the

1

humanitarianism of José Clemente Orozco, the experimental phenomenon of Pablo Picasso, the challenging individualism of Frank Lloyd Wright, and the emotional introspection of Paul Klee.

Certainly the architects and the painters have enjoyed considerable attention by the historians from this point of view. The increasing inventiveness and productivity of the sculptors during the past ten years, combined with the more general recognition of their value and actual necessity in the new stylistic pattern established by contemporary architecture, present a challenge which suggests endless possibilities of development. The attempt here, therefore, is to present in as complete a form as possible the ideas and achievements of this one sculptor who, at the age of seventy-five is creatively producing at a rate equal to the revolutionary success of his early period.

It has been a continuous process. He was beset from early youth with large ideas which had been inspired in turn by the century-long folk ambitions of his countrymen toward freedom from oppression, and he was determined—with his own bare hands if need be—to do something toward their accomplishment. At the age of fifty, in his introductory remarks for an illustrated volume on his work published by *Nova Evropa* in Zagreb, he expressed the feeling that his were little more than preparatory studies: "Almost all the works here reproduced must be regarded as mere jottings and sketches for subsequent more finished works which have never been achieved. I have the feeling that my best work will remain forever hidden and unhewn in the pure granite which lies at the heart of the mountain."

Ivan Meštrović has frequently spoken of his peasant origin in the poverty-stricken mountains of Dalmatia and has always considered it one of his greatest assets. "Poverty and need are often the most precious of inheritances, for a poor man cannot be cast down any further even by the greatest of failures." He accepted the fate of his environment and knew it to be his duty to do what he could to sow a few seeds on the wasted soil of his homeland.

Possessed himself of a strong and stubborn individuality, this sense of duty is closely associated with the artist's creative independence. "We can and must be satisfied with our own modes of expression," he advised his fellow artists in the same article; ". . . we must be conscious of the duty before us to ennoble both ourselves and those around us. The poorer the environment the more sacred the duty."

Ours is a highly mechanized and materialistic age which, in spite of its great accomplishments, seems forever in need of the sympathetic ear of the psychiatrist. For, he says at another point in the same essay, "in no age has so much been talked and written about individuality as in the present one and in no age have these qualities been so visibly lacking." The tendency is strong to allow liberty to be defined by mass opinion, and progress determined by the appetites of the many. But a few will follow Christ's example and seek after the eternal things. "We peasants," he says, "who have learned to follow the plow . . . hope that the harvest time will give us wheat, or at least enough grain for seed. We must have faith."

At another point he firmly agrees with those who hold that "art must be free from the tyranny of autocracy, the vulgarity of democracy and the dogma of religion; I can well believe that the nameless craftsmen who built the cathedrals of France did so of their own free will and conviction, and that all true artists, both before and since, who have faith in their work, have toiled as gladly as they. It is precisely the presence of this faith that has guided me in my borrowings from national and biblical history."

In an interview published by the Croatian periodical *Hrvatska Revija* twenty years later (September 1953), on the occasion of his seventieth birthday, this philosophy is changed only by its greater depth and perspective.

"I remember that my grandfather and father when they were the age I am today used to tell me: 'Where have the years and life itself gone?' And now I am asking the same question about the swift passage of time. I am not disturbed that my accumulated years herald the not too far distant end, for mere physical existence does not have much attraction and man perseveres through it by some sense of duty. Occasionally though, I am disturbed by the question: 'What has your life in its totality amounted to, and in particular what have you accomplished of the things you dreamed and strove after? How much of the blame falls on yourself, and how much on circumstance, that you have accomplished only a minute part of what you aspired to do?'

"At forty, this question came to me for the first time, but I consoled myself, that I still had time to accomplish more. At fifty this question disturbed me more deeply. By the age of sixty I became convinced that a man cannot raze mountains, and now at seventy, I have become resigned and I console myself with the thought: 'Do still what you can and as much as you can, for the journey's end is near at hand.'

"Despite everything, reason tells me that I need not lament my fate, for other men like me have lived through the same misfortunes. I cannot and I will not complain about the world. . . . An artist by the very nature of his call is a stranger whether he live in exile or in his native land, and he must accept his fate and find his *chez soi* within himself. But throughout life I carried with me an incomparable inheritance, poverty: poverty of my family and my nation. The first helped me never to be afraid of material difficulties, for I knew I could never have less than at the beginning. The second drove me to persevere in my work, so that at least in my own field my nation's poverty

3

would be diminished. I always heard deep within myself a whisper saying: 'My poor, small homeland, in the entire world you are the greatest and the dearest to my heart.' This feeling enabled me to accomplish a few things of value in my life. No matter how far fate has blown the frail tree of my life across foreign lands, its roots have always sucked nourishment from that little barren clod of soil from which it sprung."

These ideas, which he expressed with modesty and conviction in 1933 and again in 1953, contain essentially the credo of Meštrović. It has proved an enduring creed which neither war, nor adversity, nor yet success could change, and which has taken on increased significance in the years of ideological conflict which followed the Second World War.

That Meštrović is a major figure in the sculpture of the twentieth century there can be no question. Indeed the judgment of time will place him among the great sculptors of history. Tradition has meaning. The elder brother of the Yugoslav King Alexander, Prince Djordje Karadjordjević, who was a devoted friend of Meštrović and had also known Rodin in the early years of the First World War, once asked the aging master who would take his place. "Don't worry" replied Rodin, "your Meštrović is greater than I."

The point of this comment, made in an interview with Prince Djordje in 1957, is not to engage in idle superlatives, but to emphasize this artist's profound respect for the past which had led him long ago to the realization that art is a medium for the expression of ideas rather than the idea itself. His own mode of expression he seems to have found even before he entered the Academy, as will be shown later, and the process of experimentation in the various aesthetic problems of contemporary art—the new content—was simply not in his area of interest.

The judgment of Meštrović's work in the end is not a matter of competition, since he has steadfastly refused to compete with his contemporaries, but rather the degree to which he has been able to accomplish what he set out to do. These objectives have been high, indeed on the heights of the great sculptural achievements of western man from Rodin and Michelangelo to the classics of medieval Europe, ancient Greece, and Egypt. On that score he has been the most modest, severe, even bitter critic of his own work, since life is short, human limitations are great and his ambitions have been high.

To review fifty years of Meštrović's work in the public arena of the international exhibitions and museums, the criticism of the press, the published monographs, and the commissioned public monuments of Europe and America is a fascinating story which encompasses the entire history of the twentieth century. In that arena the great sculptors were all active, led by the towering Rodin and surrounded by an older group including Meunier,

4

Maillol, Bourdelle, Milles, Brancusi, Barlach and Lehmbruck. Along with Meštrović is a younger and more individual group including such personalities as Epstein, Zorach, Laurens, Belling, Archipenko and Lipchitz.

In the case of Meštrović's relationship with other artists or critics, there is little of the controversial and vindictive to be found in his writing or even conversation. He has remained singularly unconcerned with the usual arguments concerning the conservative as opposed to the progressive artists, since they in truth have little to do with the determination of his position in twentieth-century sculpture. Meštrović has always maintained a deep respect for other artists—if they were genuine—and they in turn have long respected him. In America this has been especially true, as Alonzo Lansford said in the *Art Digest* review of April 15 of the Meštrović show of 1947 at the Metropolitan Museum. "It is singularly significant that he is almost unanimously revered by American sculptors of all schools as one of the greatest living sculptors."

Auguste Rodin's oft-quoted comment, that "Meštrović was the greatest phenomenon among the sculptors" of his time, is to be understood from this point of view. He had qualities which were common to many of the great artists of our century, but he had others that set him very definitely apart. Born of solid peasant stock, he had the strong, stubborn individuality and directness, as well as an endless capacity for hard work, which one generally finds with those who have been reared in contact with the soil. He had technical skill and an innate sense of form, sometimes called artistic talent, which, in combination with individuality, form the indispensable prerequisites of the sculptor. Though his formal education was limited, he had ideas—large ideas—which could easily be ridiculed as the product of romantic nineteenth-century *Weltschmerz* idealism. And yet in his case these had a grim and desperate reality supported by the centuries-long oppression of his Croatian people. Out of need and poverty sprang a sense of duty, not to himself, but to humanity, which over the years took on a deeply rooted religious intensity.

In the arena of public art he stood apart from the stylistic groups and their various nationalistic affiliations. He was neither an impressionist nor an expressionist. Though he studied, worked and exhibited in Austria, Italy, France, England and the United States, he cannot be classified as belonging to one or another, and yet he has been a part of all of these nationalities, their traditions and their faiths. He was a Croatian, and what he tried to express was rooted in the heart and soil of his homeland. Its successful achievement, however, was not in the one language, but rather in that of all humanity.

II

Ivan Meštrović was born August 15, 1883 in the little village of Vrpolje, in the Sava valley of Croatia in the northern part of what is now Yugoslavia, where his father had sought seasonal work. Ivan was the eldest in a family of ten children of whom six survived. A few months later the family was back home in the Croatian village of Otavice, in the Dalmatian Alps not far from the market town of Drniš. That area is one of the poorest sections of a traditionally grim and forbidding mountainous country. The father was a farmer and mason, whose daily activities alternated between the plowing and harvesting of the fields, the care of the flocks, the building of houses, and the patriarchal guidance of a large family. By tradition the father's ancestors had been *hajduk* fighters, outlaws of the type of Robin Hood, which through the generations was the only defense the subjugated Croatian and Serbian people had against the harsh rule of their Turkish masters.

As a boy, Ivan had his share of the family tasks of tending the sheep and working in the fields, but he took less interest in this than in the activity of mallet and chisel associated with the building and simple decoration of the stone houses of the peasant community. His marked skill and fascination with stone carving were evident at an early age, so that the Giotto-type legend concerning the artist's origin as a peasant shepherd boy which is repeated so often about great artists of the past has a very genuine and factual meaning in the case of Ivan Meštrović.

Under these circumstances the educational opportunities for the boy in a formal sense were limited. Among the villagers his father was the only one who could read and write. The home, with a pious and devoted mother and a craftsman father cultivated in the folk traditions of his people, found its chief sources of inspiration and spiritual development in the Bible and the large body of the historic ballads which everyone knew by heart. For the artist whose eventual horizons were extended to the great cultural centers of Europe and America, whose knowledge of people and languages became that of an international citizen, this circumstance of basic orientation rather than formal education is significant to the understanding of his career.

The parents took pride in the boy's artistic accomplishments. It was a long journey on foot when his father took him to the outside world for the first time to the neighboring seacoast town of Šibenik. Two things made a deep impression on him there, as he later recalled. One was the Cathedral of St. Jacob with its stone sculpture and marvelous heads of white marble, said to be portraits of the stone carvers themselves—the work of the old masters! The other was the sea with its luminous blue color and wide, endless expanse

6

as only seen on the Dalmatian shore of the Adriatic.

The boy's reputation as a sculptor soon grew beyond the limits of his home village. There is a story of a prosperous and educated landowner of Drniš who requested the fourteen-year-old boy to carve a small figure of Christ. Within a week Meštrović returned with the completed figure. With condescending generosity the man held out a silver florin in payment. Although the boy knew little of the value of money at the time, he was well aware that his effort was worth much more than that. He refused the payment and ran away. Thus pride in workmanship had its parallel in the personal dignity and self-respect of the artist. Although the episode in itself is of no great significance, it reveals something of the strong individuality which helped to shape the particular character of his later career both as an artist and as a patriot.

It was with the meager savings of his father and the help of some of the elders of the village that the young artist was taken to Split and apprenticed to Pavle Bilinić, a stone cutter, whose workshop produced the usual grave memorials, altars and church decorations of this somewhat larger community. He stayed there less than a year, and though only a youth of fifteen years, he distinguished himself by his ability to carve a figure directly from the stone without relying on the mechanical process of developing it from a model by pointing. With the general level of the shopwork based on the literal reproduction of provincial Italian sculpture models, it was relatively easy to be noticed. As he once said of this and similar situations, "even the most modest tree is easily noticeable where there is no forest."

Through the medium of a retired army officer by the name of Captain Grubišić, a Viennese mine owner named Koenig became interested enough in the young artist to finance his trip to Vienna to study art at the Academy. The change was dramatic, and difficult, for here were all the resources of a great cultural metropolis—the old masters in the museum, the famous monuments of classical antiquity, and the Vienna Academy of Fine Arts. The language, moreover, was German of which Meštrović did not speak one word. He was dressed in the peasant's traditional clothes of his home district. He had no drawings, diploma or certificates as emblems of formal training necessary for him to be considered for entrance into the Academy. Thus for the time being, at least, the doors were closed.

For several months Meštrović lived with a Czech family by the name of Sycora, who helped him with his German, gave him a modest space to work, and arranged for him to meet a retired sculpture professor from the Vienna Kunstgewerbeschule, Otto Koenig (1838-1920). Trained in Dresden and a specialist primarily in figurines and the more commercial decorative arts,

7

Koenig agreed, somewhat reluctantly at first, to assist the youth in his preparation for the entrance examinations for the Academy. Meštrović worked in Koenig's studio for seven months. Proceeding through a series of steps, first a copy of one of Koenig's small pieces, then copies from antique sculpture, several eighteenth-century heads and finally a portrait head of Koenig from nature, the artist was thus able to demonstrate both his technical skill in following an accepted model and his own ability to work directly from nature and produce an original work of art.

Otto Koenig had no great and favorable reputation among the academy sculptors, but he did manage a review of Meštrović's work by Edmund Hellmer, director of the Academy. What convinced Hellmer more than anything else was, according to the story, the decidedly un-Koeniglike head of Koenig as executed by his young pupil. A free copy of Michelangelo's early *Pietà* and several other independent head studies clearly revealed Meštrović's individual approach, so that Hellmer readily agreed to the examination and the young sculptor was accepted. He then followed the regular four-year curriculum, working in the beginning with the sculptors Hellmer and Hans Bitterlich, and later with the architect Otto Wagner. Though he received small sums of money from various Croatian student organizations in Vienna, and later the municipality of Drniš and the Society of Croatian artists in Zagreb, he was obliged to rely on his own resources for his main support. This he did by copying paintings of old masters in the Hof Museum and by occasional commissions.

The understanding of character in an artist's work is often more readily available in the study of his early career, particularly when the account, as is necessary in most cases, is based on his own comments and narrative. The natural tendency over the years is to recall the events and ideas which have particular meanings in a given context. These grow in importance as the situations accumulate and expand into ever-widening experiences. Strong and sensitive as the young artist was, his reactions were invariably immediate and positive. Background, character and experience are therefore fused into a courageous individuality which became one of the distinguishing characteristics of his total career.

To be accepted by an academy of art required the ability to conform to certain technical and stylistic conventions, as well as the independence of character to develop beyond the mere formula of convention. Vienna and the Academy, however, represented for Meštrović a larger problem of an individual's adjustment to society and its conventions as well as the artist's relationship to traditional modes of expression. Here it was not a question of one master and one point of view, but many ideas from which the young

8

creative individual chooses or rejects according to his own particular needs. As Meštrović saw it, the artistic level of the Academy was not high, and the work of its professors a weak and conventional neobaroque. Their influence on his development was therefore minor, and the significance of the Academy lay chiefly in the fact that as an institution it provided models and a place to work, and afforded the opportunity to study copies of Greek statues and a good library of art books.

No artist, however, has ever developed in a vacuum and the artistic milieu of Vienna and central Europe in 1900-1904 had many facets of both subject matter and form which provided a background whose significance is often ignored in the study of contemporary art. There were two sculptors with whom Meštrović came into direct contact at the Academy. One was Edmund Hellmer, a Vienna Academy graduate who in 1894 had executed the victory monument commemorating the successful defense of Vienna against the Turks in 1683, located in St. Stephen's Cathedral. He is also responsible for many public monuments, such as the *Goethe* on the *Opernring* (1900) in Vienna and *Johann Strauss* in the city park. The style represents a gradual change from reserved classic to a pompous, and exceedingly dull decorative baroque. In 1900 Hellmer published *Lehrjahre in Der Plastik*, which emphasized the solid foundation of the sculptor in craftsmanship and the study of nature.

The second was Hans Bitterlich, a younger sculptor, author of the Gutenberg Monument in Vienna (1900) who was appointed professor at the Academy in 1901. Like the other professors who were proud of their own German origin, he was not particularly enthusiastic about "the glory of evoking genius in an unknown Croatian peasant. . . . You already have a style," he told the boy. "I could have no influence over you." Meštrović vividly recalls Director Hellmer's formal presentation of Professor Bitterlich to the students, and the announcement by Bitterlich that he would continue to give new depth and vigor to the German character of the Vienna Academy. "Then why don't you teach in Berlin?" was the prompt question of the Croatian peasant; whereupon Director Hellmer had a difficult time re-establishing the discipline of proper student-faculty relationship. In general, Meštrović did not agree with the criticism of his work and in the end, he was simply allowed to work on his own without interference.

During his last year Meštrović attended the architectural design class of Otto Wagner (1841-1918), the leading creative personality of the Academy and a pioneer in the development of modern architecture in Austria. Wagner's influence was of a more inspiring and general nature, not only on Meštrović but on art in all central Europe. Though essentially an architect, he

9

had been a regular participant in exhibitions with designs for textiles, furniture, book binding, ceramics, even iron grilles and lighting fixtures. He had been a leader (1900-1905) in the Vienna Secession group, the *Vereinigung Bildender Künstler Oesterreichs,* which had been established a few years before (1897) as an exhibition outlet for the younger and more progressive artists who were outside the closed circle of the government-supported academicism. Through his own work (the Vienna Technological Museum, 1907, the new Academy of Fine Arts and University Library, both in Vienna, 1910), and that of his students, notably Josef Olbrich and Josef Hoffman, architect and famous director of the *Wiener Werkstätte,* Wagner was a major influence on the creation of Vienna as one of Europe's most significant centers of design and production in the modern decorative arts for more than a generation.

To this background might be credited Meštrović's interest and competence in architectural design, with regard to both architectural form itself and its decorative embellishment, as seen later in the Kossovo project and the Račić memorial. Meštrović's approach to the many architectural projects he had occasion to do in later years was always that of a sculptor, with the sculptor's sense of monumental form, a simple straightforward, elemental mass. His sculptural decoration was an integrated development from the basic form, either as a cleancut relief with its major emphasis on the surface, or as three-dimensional sculpture which is usually in direct relationship to the surrounding space created by the architecture.

There are several other features of this background of central Europe in 1900-1910 which suggest, not direct influences on the art of Meštrović, but rather, much of the cultural milieu against and through which the young artist reacted. The significance of Meštrović as one of the great personalities of twentieth century art, and indeed as one of the great masters in the history of sculpture, must be understood from this point of view.

Even the most casual glance through the German-language magazines dealing with contemporary art of that time will reveal an amazing variety of forms and ideas, a remarkable creative vitality, and a general tendency toward the integration of these ideas into the total fabric of society as a functioning and genuinely twentieth-century style.

This was not the product of official patronage, but rather the agitation of progressive-minded individuals and groups outside the government-sponsored academies and educational institutions. It was rooted in the experimental individualism of Paris, particularly the French painters, and developed through various channels—*Art Nouveau* in France and the Low Countries, Secession in the organized groups of Berlin, Munich and Vienna

—largely under the leadership of the architects who sought to apply these new ideas of design to their practical problems of gracious living for the great middle class portion of society now attracting their attention.

The new art was basically social in nature. A lead article with a familiar ring, "Luxury Art or People's Art" (Luxuskunst oder Volkskunst) in Die Kunst for December 1901 challenged the artist to think in terms of the essential, genuine and functional values of the many, rather than those of the precious upper few. Extensive and continuous articles appeared on Peter Behrens and his fertile experimentation in new materials and design, on the inspiring work of the Scotsman, Charles Mackintosh, and on Otto Wagner and his many pupils. Continuously stressed was the extension of the new design from architecture and painting to every article of the living ensemble: furniture, stained glass, mosaics, lighting fixtures, ceramics, metalwork, jewelry, even embroidery, bookbinding and printing. Indeed, such a revolutionary and universal reform in the design of all objects did not occur again until a generation later.

Considerable prominence is given to the painters and the progressive ideas of style and subject matter they reflect. Ignoring the pedantic and banal realism of the academies which persisted as a legacy from the nineteenth century, there was deep respect for the older French contemporaries, notably the Impressionists, the solid Courbet, and the new developments of Gauguin, Puvis de Chavannes and Toulouse-Lautrec.

There was the usual emphasis on the contemporary Germans, though not in an obnoxiously nationalistic way. Franz von Lenbach was still a strong tradition, but the general point of view emphasized the personal expression of the artist through the individualized study of nature and the intensive development of the new and permanent values uncovered by the school of Paris, particularly the Impressionists. Thus a great variety of personalities appear with persistent regularity: Hans von Marees, Wilhelm Trübner, Max Liebermann, Lovis Corinth, Max Slevogt, Arnold Böcklin, Ferdinand Hodler and Franz von Stuck. They vary from a direct commitment to Impressionist technique, such as that of Max Liebermann, to the more expressive and dynamic brush work of Corinth and Slevogt, and the large figures and heavy symbolism of Böcklin, Hodler and Stuck. All emphasize color, but the more radical and abstract experiments of the Brücke and Blaue Reiter groups had not yet been raised to prominence.

The importance given to drawing and the monumental figure was directly related to the continued interest in content and the necessity for communication through the medium of symbolism or historic narrative. To the traditional religious and historical themes carried over from the nineteenth cen-

11

tury are added the often elaborate symbolism based on classical and contemporary literature (such as Gerhart Hauptmann) usually with moral or patriotic implications. A steady undercurrent in this pre-Expressionist period was therefore a strong movement toward a new combination of monumental form and significant content, which in history seems best accomplished through the medium of sculpture.

Indeed, great expectations appear in the accounts of the sculptors. In an article on Ernst Barlach published in *Die Kunst* in November 1901, Karl Scheffler expressed the hope that the search for new forms of expression noted in contemporary painting would soon develop in sculpture.

The sculptors, to be sure, had more than their rightful share of the banalities of everyday realism and prescribed subject matter. Hellmer's seated figure of Goethe, mentioned before, with his large head, protruding stomach, outspread knees and slumped posture on his big throne is characteristically dreary. No less so is Max Klinger's grim, gaudy and frightening monument to Beethoven with its many-colored marble and naked, fist-pounding classic figure of the great composer which was exhibited in the large Klinger show at the Vienna Secession in 1902.

Foreign sculptors were not much better. Albert Bartholomé's *Monument Aux Mortes* in the Père Lachaise cemetery of Paris—an Egyptian pylon-type monument with a frieze of emaciated and very naked mourning figures across the base—was featured in the German press in 1899. A special exhibition of sculpture of the recently deceased Constantin Meunier (d. 1906) was held in the Keller and Reiner Galleries of Berlin, featuring his *Monument to Work* with realistic reliefs of miners, harvesters, dockworkers and single figures of the miner, the sower and other workman types. American sculpture received similar attention in an article respectfully featuring Daniel Chester French, Homer Saint Gaudens and George Gray Barnard.

Recognition of the great potentialities of contemporary sculpture appeared in the articles on Auguste Rodin. A review of his work by Paul Clemen was published in *Die Kunst* for April 1905. In it Rodin was hailed as the greatest sculptor of France, even though he had been alternately praised and excommunicated by his public for many years. A large retrospective exhibition of his work was held in a special pavilion at the Paris World's Fair of 1900, followed by others in the principal capitals of Europe, including Vienna.

The contrast between the truly great and inspiring sculpture of Rodin and the endless variety of nationalistic monuments which appeared, not only in Germany but all over Europe, is striking. Monuments to the national, political, military and literary heroes, as well as war memorials, appear in almost every park and square. Often it is size rather than stature which is the determining factor. In the tradition of the classic Athena of the Parthenon appear the gigantic goddesses of *Bavaria* in Munich, the *Niederwald Denkmal* on the Rhine and the French-American *Statue of Liberty*. A Munich Secession show of 1903 featured Hugo Kaufmann's model for the *Vaterland-slied* destined for Frankfurt, a bronze warrior group with singing minstrel commemorating the unification of Germany.

The list is endless, but perhaps the most extensive monument of the type is the towering *Battle of Nations* memorial (*Völkerschlachtdenkmal*) near Leipzig which was built in 1906-1913 with Bruno Schmitz, a pupil of Otto Wagner, as architect and Franz Metzner (1870-1919) as sculptor. Metzner was a self-taught sculptor who had originally been trained as a stonemason and had been professor of sculpture at the Vienna *Kunstgewerbeschule* for a short time (1903-1906) before settling in Berlin. His was an attempt to develop a type of symbolic expression freed from the physical limitations of the human figure. The result is a kind of abstract symbolism such as Will, Energy, Suffering, and Struggle, which is imparted by highly stylized figures, some of them inflated to excessive size and empty pathos.

In the spring exhibition of the Vienna Secession of 1904, Metzner showed the model for the *Niebelungen* fountain intended for the city of Vienna: a single armored figure with folded arms and a mass of softly flowing, inter-woven figures crouching below. A twisted male figure in bronze with sharply bent head and bulging, elongated muscles, entitled *Earth* appeared in the same show and revealed both the influence of Rodin and the characteristic literary symbolism of the period.

This brief review is not intended as a history of the Art Nouveau or Secession movement in the early twentieth century, but rather as a suggestion of something of the cultural climate into which the young Meštrović came and through which he developed. When a complete history of this movement is written from the all-European point of view it will be one of the basic and most important studies of the art of our times, and it will show that in the end Meštrović contributed much more to it than he received from it. It will show, furthermore, that the new art, which we in mid-century are pleased to call contemporary, did in fact have its beginning as an integrated social and cultural movement at that early date and would have accomplished its objectives long ago had it not been for the destructive interruptions of two world wars.

Along with the bubbling ferment of new ideas is to be noted the deeply rooted nationalism which does not always rear its head as an ugly and predatory monster. In the right hands it can become a genuinely inspiring and creative force. The international example of the progressive Rodin provided the artistic means for its expression. And while there were many who caught the spirit, it was Meštrović who seemed to embody the union of the two.

The many-centuried cry for freedom and deliverance, which Meštrović had learned through the plaintive ballads of the Serbo-Croatian *guslari* was a very practical matter in 1900. The Balkan peoples were seething in revolt against the Turks, and within the Austro-Hungarian Empire the Croatians and Serbians were struggling to resist political domination, the cultural encirclement, and eventual annihilation threatened by their German-Hungarian masters. The promise of equal status for the Yugoslav minority groups within a hoped-for federation of the empire was never fulfilled, and the issues which the young Croatian patriot-sculptor faced as a student in the empire's capital city, remained vital and penetrating throughout his career.

By 1904 a much more mature young sculptor had learned that nationalism was a larger phenomenon which involved entire races, creeds and traditions. In the hands of the small and selfish it becomes a means of control and enslavement. In the hands of the genuinely creative it becomes an instrument for the liberation of the spirit and the mutual understanding of all mankind. This conviction, profound to the point of a religious faith, Meštrović has always maintained as a basic philosophy.

Meštrović was a producing sculptor though still a student at the Academy and under twenty-one during this first period, 1900-1904. Well over twenty-five full-scale pieces are recorded during those four years, including portraits, saints, religious subjects, nude figures, and original compositions. The story is told that as a second-year student he had carved a full-sized mother and child which, though thoroughly competent and therefore impossible to eliminate from the annual student show, nevertheless had a certain rather brutal and naked quality which caused some consternation in the exhibition committee as to the propriety of exhibiting it. To avoid embarrassment, therefore, the figure was placed to one side of the hall behind a curtain.

Needless to say the reaction was immediate and the realistic mother received much more attention than if she had been given the most conspicuous place in the hall. The members of the Secession, ever on the alert for the nonconformist who showed promise, invited him to exhibit with their group, and in the following year he was accepted as a member of the society and a regular exhibitor.

The realism of the young Croatian was not the usual fidelity to nature but rather an additional movement, somewhat heavy and awkward, but carrying a genuine peasant strength. This is the quality which appears developed in the sorrowing Widows of the Kossovo group several years later. It is no accident that in these same early years he should be attracted to the bearded, brooding character of Count Tolstoi, a half-length figure of whom Meštrović modeled in 1904. The ideals of Tolstoi stressing the dignity of labor, the peasant, and the men of the soil were popular among artists and liberals of the time, and portraits of him in the characteristic long beard and peasant shirt were featured in the popular art periodicals.

A major work, and the one which provided the means for the development of a new phase of the artist's career, was the plaster model for the *At the Well of Life* which was exhibited in the Secession Building in 1904. Around the cylindrical form of the fountain are woven life-size pairs of nude figures — Love, Youth, and Old Age — thirsting for the Water of Life. It was purchased by Karl Wittgenstein, a well-to-do iron mine owner, to be cast in bronze and used as a garden piece for his home in Vienna. In 1910 the piece was purchased by the city of Zagreb and placed in the square in front of the National Theater (Figs. 1 and 2).

Wittgenstein subsequently commissioned Meštrović to execute a second fountain, *At the Source of Life* (Fig. 3), for the entrance vestibule of his home. This is a wall group carved directly in high relief from a single block of black Belgian granite, representing cowering pairs of male and female figures on either side, a row of *putti* across the back with the water spurting from a huge breast at the top. Wittgenstein also commissioned Meštrović to do a half-figure portrait of his wife.

The proceeds from these sales and a few smaller pieces also purchased by Wittgenstein provided the financial means to travel, first to see Italy and Michelangelo's work, and then to Paris and the inspiring atmosphere of that internationally recognized center of contemporary art. More than that, however, these two groups represent a turning point in his artistic career. For recognition instills confidence, and the fact that one man was willing to pay money for the curiously different work of an unknown student sculptor from the provinces seemed justification enough for the artist to go ahead with his own ideas.

The trend of his thinking can be seen by comparing these two fountain designs. The first is more conventional, that is, conventional in terms of the then radical Auguste Rodin and his tortured lost souls in the *Gate of Hell*. The second is more monumental with its full-size figures cowering with brutal shame and fear almost as though guilty of the original sin. As a matter of fact, the artist was working on two such full-length figures of Adam and Eve at the same time, so the related symbolism was not accidental.

Meštrović continued to exhibit in the Secession; some of the work he had done as a student, others he had executed on frequent visits to Split. The two fountains were described and reproduced in critical reviews of the Secession show. Several compositions with a challenging content appeared: the *Timor*

Dei (1904), a sculpture of an enormous naked foot, powerful with tense muscles and cramped toes crushing a mass of writhing naked figures. Another was a relief depicting the Slavic legend, *Building of Skadar,* in which by the will of fate a woman of the village was to be buried in the walls. To insure the survival of her children to the last possible moment, the masons allowed holes to remain in the walls so that the children might suckle at her breasts until death.

The implications were well understood and appreciated in the press comments. The motif of the *Timor Dei,* related to Rodin's *Hand of God,* was interpreted both as political oppression and the fate of mankind. The legend of Skadar was associated with the fountain of life theme, stressing not oppression, but the divine quality of mother love, faithful to the death, which remains forever the foundation and strength of nations and of peoples. Thus too, the traditional religious theme of a mother nursing her child takes on a rededicated significance in the direct and realistic medium of Meštrović.

A review of the 1906 spring Secession exhibition in Vienna in *Die Kunst* for June 1906 prominently reproduced *At the Well of Life* and stressed this universal symbolism. It pointed to Meštrović as an already established young sculptor who had executed a monument to the popular Croatian poet Luka Botić in Split. Here was no suggestion of condescension toward the provincial peasant, but rather a deep respect for his Croatian nationality and his sense of cultural mission.

III

The ten years after the academy (1904-1914) might well be called the Kossovo period. It brought the crystallization of Meštrović's ideas in sculptural form, their exhibition in the major capitals of Europe and the artist's recognition as one of the foremost sculptors of our time.

In 1904 Meštrović spent several months in Italy, then went to Paris where he conceived and developed the first phase of the vast Kossovo monument. By 1905 he had already completed several figures for this undertaking which were exhibited in the Salon d'Automne. The aged and kindly Rodin took a keen interest in the young man and invited him to visit his studio. Thus began a close friendship which Meštrović treasured through the years, not as a stylistic influence any longer, but as guiding inspiration for the many projects now going through his mind.

Large projects are often predestined to failure. The very magnitude of a

16

conception creates obstacles to achievement. The Kossovo monument was for Meštrović a great dream rooted in the folk literature of his people. The plan was for a temple, a pantheon to commemorate the battle of Kossovo and the heroes who died there. And, although for this ambitious undertaking the artist could find no financial support, undeterred he proceeded to create individual pieces of the projected whole.

Kossovo is a fifty-mile long plain in Serbia. Its melancholy and dramatic interest to the Yugoslavs is the fact that it was the scene of the crushing defeat, on June 20, 1389, of the Serbian forces under Tsar Lazar I by the Turks under Sultan Murad I. Through five hundred years of suppression and enslavement the memory of Kossovo was kept alive in the minds and hearts of the people through countless popular ballads and folk songs sung by wandering minstrels, the *guslari*, who told of the heroic exploits of Tsar Lazar, Marko Kraljević, Banović Strahinja, Miloš Obilić, Srdja Zlopogledja, and the countless maidens and mothers who suffered as a result of the Kossovo catastrophe.

The plan of the proposed temple was essentially an octagonal central building covered by domical vaults. Square chapels covered by octagonal vaults were to extend on three sides. A long atrium with a massive pylonlike facade dramatized the entrance. The various motifs of steeds, lions, spears and falcons decorating the facade are from the folk songs, especially the *Mother of the Jugovići*. The main corridor of the atrium was to be flanked by over life-size caryatids whose stern, priestesslike character symbolizes the nation's fate. Reliefs of battle scenes were to cover the walls behind the caryatids. At the end of the corridor was to be the Great Sphinx, a powerful, winged figure symbolizing the riddle of destiny. Over this, crowning the entrance into the temple proper, was conceived a "tower of the sacrificed" in the form of an obelisk of five superimposed rows of winged angels.

The massive hall itself was to have a seated figure of the blind *gusle*-player, the wandering singer of folk songs, as the symbol of the artist through whom the richness and power of a people's collective experience finds expression. Around this monumental space, and in the adjoining chambers were to be figures of the great heroes, Marko Kraljević, Miloš Obilić, Srdja Zlopogledja, Banović Strahinja, and the series of Widows who symbolize the sorrow and lament for sacrificed heroes.

Marko Kraljević (Fig. 6) was perhaps the most colorful of the Kossovo heroes. The son of a fourteenth-century Serbian king, and a handsome child-like hero of prodigious strength, he was Prince of Prilep in Macedonia and a vassal of the Turks. Though he did not take part in the Battle of Kossovo, the popular ballads developed him into a legendary hero, a chivalrous Hercules, a rebel and protector of downtrodden people.

17

Of almost equal importance is his swift and powerful, great-necked, pie-bald steed, Šarac, who understood the human tongue and shared his master's heroic exploits. Through the centuries, according to the legend, Marko slept in a cave guarded by mountain spirits, with his great sword thrust deep into solid rock, to await the hand of a deliverer.

Another hero, Miloš Obilić, having fallen into the disfavor of his father-in-law, Tsar Lazar, due to the intrigues of his enemies, attempted to prove his loyalty by cutting his way through the Turkish ranks and slaying the Sultan Murad with his own hand. In the legend Miloš was the symbol of action and revenge, who would seize the sword of Marko from the rock and lead his people to liberty.

Banović Strahinja (Fig. 8) appears only infrequently in the Kossovo ballads, but then as strong and beautiful in body, hence the restriction of Meštrović's figure to the torso form.

From their distant and uncertain origin these legends were handed down orally and, as mentioned before, Meštrović's father knew an extraordinary number which he sang at home in Otavice. Though the major portion was of the heroic and epic type, there was a large number of lyric songs of love and pleasure which were sung not only at dances and celebrations, but also at work in the fields.

Meštrović loved to tell these stories to his family and friends. One of his favorites was *The Mother of the Jugovići* which had been the subject of a famous drama by Count Ivo Vojnović and which was the theme Meštrović had used for a seated figure of the mother, sorrowfully gazing at the hand of her dead son (1908). A second was the story of the Battle of Kossovo and Tsar Lazar whose fateful choice of the heavenly rather than the earthly kingdom sent his soldiers to defeat and death at the hands of the Turks.

The first sketches for the Kossovo monument were made in Vienna in 1905 and 1906. But the main Kossovo figures were modeled in Paris during the next two years. In the annexation of Bosnia-Herzegovina in 1908 Meštrović saw another national catastrophe, a further attempt by Austria-Hungary to seal forever the tragic division of his people. This sent him back to the Kossovo figures with renewed determination. Thus in less than two years of furious work Meštrović was ready for his first major exhibition. This occurred in 1909 in the Vienna Secession where he showed a group of over fifty pieces of which the majority were associated with the Kossovo project.

The reaction was immediate and enthusiastic by both art critics and historians, such as the eminent Arthur Roessler and Josef Strzygowski. They praised the power, originality, and technical mastery of both figure and material. They could classify the twenty-four-year-old sculptor only as a "phe-

18

nomenon." But with his explosive type of subject matter, some were fearful of his work as "propaganda."

At the close of the exhibition several figures—*Memories* (Fig. 13), *Widows* (Fig. 11) and the *Widow with Child* (Fig. 16)—were marked for purchase for the government Belvedere Museum. This purchase, however, was rejected at the personal order of none other than the Archduke Franz Ferdinand, who was opposed to the Yugoslav nationalism which Meštrović's sculpture embodies. As it happened, the rejection was more to the advantage of the artist and the Yugoslav cause of national liberation than if the work had remained in the Belvedere collection. For from then until well after the First World War they served their intended patriotic purpose until the establishment of Yugoslavia was assured.

After the Vienna exhibit Meštrović returned to Zagreb where a comprehensive showing of his work was held, an exhibition which made a deep impression on his compatriots. While in his native land, to refresh his memory, his heart, and his inspiration, he did a series of portraits of his devoted mother and proud father. Their sturdy, strong and pious character had much to do with the expressive authenticity of the heroic peasant types he used. It was at this time also that he modeled a thrice life-size equestrian figure of Marko Kraljević mounted upon his horse Šarac.

In the following year (1911) the same group that had been exhibited in Zagreb together with several new pieces was shown at the International Exhibition in Rome. Here the equestrian Marko became the dominating figure in the large, domed hall which one entered through the Corridor of Caryatids (Fig. 6). This exhibition provided the occasion for the artist's greatest success. He was awarded first prize, his position as one of Europe's foremost sculptors was established, and his ideas as well as his work became the subject of international discussion.

For good or evil in Meštrović's career art and politics went hand in hand. Though the charge that he used his art as political propaganda had been hurled at him many times, Meštrović steadfastly refused to honor it with a direct reply. His work and his career provided convincing answer even at this time. In politics, business or religion, propaganda deals with an organized dogma presented through prescribed media for mass consumption. But in art one is concerned with a creative individual, and where the artist serves as a medium without personal conviction he is no longer an artist. To Meštrović this conviction was a personal dedication, amounting almost to religious faith, to his family, his people, and humanity. The concern with humanity, its tragedy and suffering is indeed the core of his religious faith, since here he sees the hope and means of salvation.

For the International Exhibition in Rome, Meštrović had been invited to exhibit in both the Austrian and Hungarian pavilions, but for patriotic reasons he refused and chose instead to join the Serbs. Since there were very few Serbian artists, what it really amounted to was a one-man show for Meštrović and the Kossovo project. In obvious competition with the Austrian and Hungarian displays, the Serbian pavilion, therefore, provided an effective rallying point for the Serbo-Croatian national movement in the explosive atmosphere of the years just preceding the assassination of Archduke Franz Ferdinand by the eighteen-year-old Yugoslav nationalist Gavrilo Princip, at Sarajevo.

The international critics hailed Meštrović as a master and one of the world's greatest sculptors. One German reviewer in the *Zeitschrift für Bildende Kunst* could not understand "why Serbia had to have a separate pavilion," but praised the master Meštrović and his figures, particularly the equestrian Marko Kraljević, for their unbelievable power, inspired grandeur and monumentality. He insisted that Kossovo would not only be a Serbian monument but an international shrine to which art lovers of the world would journey as pilgrims. "Let us hope from the bottom of our hearts," he concluded, "that he will find a patron to provide an outlet for his powerful creative strength and energy and translate his gigantic dreams into permanent stone."

Writing in the *Manchester Guardian* (June 10, 1911), the English critic James Bone was most enthusiastic about Meštrović and the Rome exhibitions. In his later comments included in the English monograph of 1919 he characterized the exhibition as a rare experience which marked the beginning of a renaissance in European sculpture. In the Kossovo series "Meštrovič concentrated and further ennobled those passionate modern strivings toward a rediscovery of the primary appeal of art. . . ." The impression he had of the 1911 exhibition proved to be a lasting one if judged by this graphic description: "As you entered the pavilion, a *loggia* of caryatides, supporting a massive tier of stone, faced you. There were six female figures on each side, partly draped, the garment following the lines of the body, but broadening at the foot to add to the strength of the structure, the type noble with its brooding brow, austere, worn, and enigmatic. The sybils might represent the centuries regarding inflexibly the sufferings of the Serbs, but each had a sense of waiting as for a great event. At one end a Sphinx, with human limbs, gazed ironically down the avenue. You passed into a domed hall large enough to contain the group of the mythic hero Marko Kraljević on his charger, about three times the size of life. The deliverer rides naked on the back of a great-necked, open-mouthed Serbian horse, short and powerful, with a huge tail. Round the hall was a frieze of panels, each with a torso in relief of a Turk or a Serbian in strong action. The arched entries on each side had a frieze of Turks' heads and the labouring bodies of captive Serbs supporting the steps. In the side halls were a series of mourning widows and heroes."

One of the most direct statements of the purpose of the project was written by Meštrović himself in 1914 and quoted by Dr. Milan Ćurčin, editor of the 1933 monograph, *Ivan Meštrović*: "What I sought to create was a synthesis of the popular national ideals and their development, to express by stone and architecture the depth of the memory of our greatest moments and the most characteristic phases of our history — forming at the same time an apex for hopes in the future, amidst nature and under the free sky. The Serbian people did not accept the defeat on the plain of Kossovo as its final fate, but only as a punishment for coming generations, who by their suffering would have to prepare the way to a new freedom — a kind of purgatory towards the final liberation. The brutal Turkish invaders defeated Tsar Lazar, the Serbian heroes and the Serbian army, and brought oppression to the country for many centuries, but they were not able to defeat the soul of the nation which remained pure and strong, ready always for another great and holy moment, to fight to the death in order to redeem justice and liberty. The leading spirit in the country, the blind *guslar,* took up the task of encouraging his fellow-countrymen, and, going from home to home, from village to village, he sang of the 'glorious defeat' strengthening in this way the faith of the people and keeping together the links of internal union, of an invisible Empire. According to the national legend, God himself gave Tsar Lazar the choice of an earthly or a heavenly kingdom, and it was the latter he chose; the *guslar* told the nation that the Tsar was not dead, but only gone over to a heavenly Empire, together with all those who were true to him and that he looks for those who remain to live and die for the same cause of final liberation. The heroes and knights, as well as later the *hajduks* and *uskoks,* or any national individuals fighting against Turk and injustice, found their way into the legends and into the soul of every Serbo-Croat peasant; they became part of his life, his consolation, and prophetic of all he thinks will come.

"The moral of those legends is simple and clear: to fight to death against oppression and cruelty, for right, for the country — no sacrifices shall be too great. From Kossovo until today this faith has lived and kept unchanged, the army of Tsar Lazar thus increasing to millions and millions. The whole of our country is an altar for this faith, and just as Tsar Lazar is the centre of the Kossovo Temple and the *guslar* his priest; so in the same way is ideally the wish for justice and progress towards the higher life of mankind the centre of the Temple, and those who proclaim them its priests. The Temple would not be dedicated to any confession or sect in particular, but to all of them, and to all of those who believe in the ideals expressed in our national legends. For this is the spirit of the nation, religious but not bigoted, a feeling that everyone who is just and honest is a 'true believer' no matter what faith he might profess."*

Though considerable emphasis has been placed on Meštrović's independence as an individual and artist from his early youth, it would be difficult to insist that he was not a part of his time. On the contrary, he did reflect the period under discussion, so deeply, in fact, that his active participation as a creative artist in contemporary political affairs had much to do with the shaping of new patterns in the succeeding period. In this he differed radically from Rodin, and it is this point likewise which distinguishes Meštrović from the contemporary European sculptors of both conservative and progressive conviction. As mentioned previously, Meštrović admired Rodin greatly and, though he never was a pupil in the formal sense and there was a considerable age difference between them, they had been good friends in Paris and Rome.

For most of the sculptors of the younger generation, Rodin was the source of a wide diversity of sculptural techniques and experimental modes of expression which paralleled the early development of modern painting. But for Meštrović, techniques and modes of expression were means to an end, not ends in themselves, and his search was for the artistic form adequate to convey the ideas which he was dedicated to express.

From the discussion in the preceding section it is evident that Meštrović's ideas had ample precedent and that the ground was particularly fertile for their development in central Europe in the tense years before the First World War. Nationalism was not a term of derision but an important, and explosive phenomenon in France and Italy as well as Germany and the Balkans. Though terrifying in its political manifestations it is basically a cultural phenomenon which found its most direct expression in literature.

As far back as the early nineteenth century, the Romantic movement — artists, philosophers, historians and the poets — had taken a deep and creative interest in the folk traditions of their respective peoples. Alongside the *Chanson de Roland,* the *Niebelungenlied,* the *Kalavala,* and the Arthurian legends, the Serbo-Croatian epic ballads of the Kossovo series had developed as a parallel source of pride and inspiration. The Germans Herder and Goethe had taken a lively interest in them and had published several translations

*The quotation is taken from Dr. Ćurčin's monograph, but changes in the translation as originally published have been made herein by Meštrović himself.

22

into German, such as Goethe's translation of the Croatian ballad *Hasana-ginica* (*Die Edle Frau von Hasan Aga*). A long line of distinguished Serbo-Croatian scholars and poets, headed by Andrija Kačić-Miošić (b. ca. 1740), Petar Petrović Njegoš (1813-1851), Luka Botić, and Joseph George Strossmayer (1815-1905) not only wrote poetry in the style of the popular ballads but helped to collect and clarify this vast literary heritage for the enjoyment and edification of their people. The man who collected and edited the folk ballads and brought them to the attention of the scholarly world was the Serb Stefan Vuk Karadžić. All of these in turn became the inspiration for many of Meštrović's most important public monuments.

Meštrović's idea of a national shrine had its precedents of varying quality and importance, from antiquity and the Roman Pantheon to its Classic Revival namesake in Paris, and the Valhalla near Regensburg. Similar projects with patriotic subject matter appeared in the work of contemporary sculptors, such as Rodin's *Citizens of Calais* and the vastly inferior monuments like Kaufmann's *Vaterlandslied* and Metzner's *Niebelungen* fountain. In the 1911 International Exhibition in Rome Meštrović was thrown into competition with the big, athletic figures of Hugo Lederer, Anton Hanak and Franz Metzner. Even at that time the critics considered the work of these men soft and ineffectual compared with the monumental strength of Meštrović's Kossovo figures.

In many of the early critical reviews Meštrović's work had been stylistically associated with two of his older contemporaries, even to the point of assuming that he had actually worked with them. One was Franz Metzner, who, it will be remembered, had lived and taught in Vienna at the *Kunstgewerbeschule* in 1903-1906 while Meštrović was at the Academy. The enthusiastic reviewer of the 1911 Rome exhibition in the *Zeitschrift für Bildende Kunst* quoted above, stated that Meštrović had studied with Metzner, but had "certainly gone his own way."

As a matter of fact, Meštrović had met the German sculptor only once at an exhibit, and even then came to a rather sharp disagreement because Metzner had criticised the work of Rodin. Meštrović regarded Metzner's work as that of an inflated ceramist and not a sculptor who works in stone.

A factual comparison of his figures with Metzner's best work — the *Masks of Fate* in the crypt and the four gigantic allegorical figures of the *Battle of Nations* monument in Leipzig — will demonstrate the truth of Meštrović's opinion. Metzner's stylized figures are huge in an artificially heroic scale with the soft, reserved pathos of tragedy and death. They reflect the quiet allegory of the sepulchre. Meštrović's figures are Warriors and Widows, often with their children, full of action and the daemonic drive characteristic of the positive faith he sees in every tragedy. "To us mortals a human tragedy is always half-divine," he later wrote, indicating again the deeply religious aspect of his conception.

Antoine Bourdelle was a second name which has been associated with Meštrović. This rumored association was proven to be untrue, but is interesting nevertheless as a reflection of the times. In the *Corriere della Serra* the Italian art critic Ugo Ojetti wrote an extremely laudatory article about Meštrović's work shown at the Rome International Exhibition in 1911. Later Ojetti asked the sculptor to give him a statue in wood for his private collection. Meštrović flatly refused saying he never offered gifts to art critics. Two years later Ojetti wrote a review about Bourdelle's exhibition in Venice saying Meštrović's *Srdja Zlopogledja* (Fig. 9) had been inspired by Bourdelle's *Heracles*. The Italian sculptor Leonardo Bistolfi, a close friend of Meštrović, was scandalized by Ojetti's assertion and attacked him in the press. Ojetti answered that he received this information from the second Mrs. Bourdelle. This moved Bistolfi and several friends to investigate the affair, and Bourdelle admitted that the assertion of Ojetti was untrue, because he had made his *Heracles* after Meštrović made his *Srdja Zlopogledja*. Bourdelle visited Meštrović's studio once in Paris and they clashed sharply because Bourdelle said that it was he who made Rodin's best works. To this Meštrović protested saying Bourdelle should tell such a tale to someone who is not a sculptor. Meštrović told the story later on to Rodin who laughed saying Bourdelle always liked to boast.

Bourdelle had designed a gigantic bronze monument to the *Defenders of 1870-1871* for Montauban (Tarn-et-Garonne), which was widely publicized when it was finished in 1900. His famous bronze archer *Heracles* of 1909 was the sensation of the Paris Salon of 1910. The Montauban war monument is distinguished for its general baroque movement, its muscular figures with their glistening play of light and shadow in the Rodin tradition. Perhaps one can see something of that character in Meštrović's youthful *At the Well of Life*, but certainly not in the Kossovo pieces he executed in Paris. Bourdelle's archer, *Heracles*, is designed again as a muscular figure, but stretched and extended into space through its long bow and wide span of arms and legs.

Meštrović had worked out the problem of the classical archer many times but in quite a different way. In his later *Cyclops* and in the equestrian Indians for Chicago, he has kept the muscular structure much more compact so that the tension has the quality of explosive power. That same compactness one certainly sees in the *Marko Kraljević* and *Banović Strahinja*. If one were to extend the comparison to the works of Maïllol one would discover

24

the same contrast in organic power which is the key to the vitality of Meštrović's heroic scale. This is not to say that one is better than the other, but that they are different. The specific purpose here is to clarify the particular character of Meštrović and to trace its development through his long and distinguished career.

One of the most revealing comparisons is to be found in two portrait busts of Rodin, done from nature by Bourdelle and Meštrović (Fig. 25). Bourdelle's famous portrait was modeled in 1910, and shows the long-bearded, short-cropped master, calm and stolid, with almost no neck and the head slightly tilted back so that it seems built directly into the shoulders. Meštrović had occasion to do a number of studies of Rodin in Rome in 1914. What he saw was not the proud Olympian, but the gaunt, heavy-featured Prophet who leans forward on his strong arms and stares intently at posterity. The subject was the same, but the artists saw differently. Meštrović's vision and expressive form were consistent with his character as it developed through this period.

Looking over the illustrations purely from a stylistic point of view, one will discover many motifs which have historical analogies in ancient Egyptian, Assyrian and Cretan civilizations. These were not necessarily his own borrowings but the common historical repertoire of the period. Thus appear the inter-weaving of modeled figures in high relief, the stretching and distortion of figures into a decorative pattern, the stylized anatomy, the twisting of figures often into anatomically impossible but nevertheless expressive poses, the use of rhythmically repeated profiles of figures in flat relief and many more. Rodin is clearly the point of departure, with Michelangelo in the background, as well as a future ideal. Others reflect Egyptian, Assyrian and ancient Cretan design motifs in the historical repertoire of the museums.

The important moment in the development of style is that in which the acquired or inherited motif loses its identity in the total design of a new expression. To the comparison of the two fountain designs, the cylindrical and the full-length figures of the fountains of the Vienna period, one might add the long-necked *Vase with Frieze of Dancers* (Fig. 19). The attenuated proportions of the figures, their curvilinear design emphasizing the roundness of protruding thigh, buttocks and abdomen, are characteristic features of Egyptian Eighteenth Dynasty figure designs of the age of Ikhnaton and Nofretete.

Compare these with the caryatids in the entrance hall of the Kossovo monument and one can discover their peculiarly enigmatic effectiveness based on the development of these same features. Neither an Athenian *Porch of the Maidens* nor the piers of an Egyptian temple, these constitute a strange invention through which a combined Christian and pagan symbolism is expressed in the monumental forms. The double line of kneeling figures flanking a winged victory, depicted in the relief of the *Kossovo Medal* in 1913, is a more literal presentation of the same basic idea.

IV

The bronze monument to *The Victor* erected in 1913 in Kalemegdan Park, Belgrade, to commemorate the Serbian victory of 1912 over the Turks in the Battle of Kumanovo would have been the beginning of a successful series of public monuments, had it not been for Sarajevo and the war. Meštrović felt it his patriotic duty to serve his country as did everyone else. The curious and significant fact, however, is that for Meštrović it meant simply continuing as a sculptor along the dedicated road he had set for himself as a boy when he left the mountain hamlet of Otavice. Now the horizons were wider, the objective more specific.

With his consistent record of opposition to the policies of the Austro-Hungarian Empire, as well as the success of his Kossovo project after the Rome exhibition, Meštrović was politically suspect. On the day Archduke Franz Ferdinand was murdered Meštrović was in Venice. That evening he took a ship to Split, where two days later an Austrian officer secretly warned him to leave the country immediately, for his arrest was imminent. The same day Meštrović escaped by boarding a ship bound for Italy just as it was leaving the pier. Thus it was that when war broke out between Austria-Hungary and Serbia, the artist was in Italy. Meštrović's father, Maté, was arrested at the beginning of the war on the charge of conspiring against Austria-Hungary. He was swiftly tried and condemned to death. Shortly before the sentence was to be carried out, however, he was reprieved and soon afterward released.

Meštrović lived in Rome, had a studio and continued to work on smaller projects, including a number of religious themes, such as the *Crucifixion*, the *Pietà, John the Baptist,* and several portraits, such as those of his friends, Leonardo Bistolfi and Auguste Rodin. It was at this time that Meštrović and two Croatian political leaders, Ante Trumbić and Frano Supilo, became worried about the future of their homeland. The exiles had been reliably informed that the Allies were secretly negotiating with Italy to enter the war on their side. As a price, Italy demanded Croat and Slovene territory on the eastern shore of the Adriatic. In order to protect Dalmatia from Italian expansion, as well as to support the cause of Yugoslav union, the exiles conceived of a Yugoslav Committee for National Liberation. Although political life as such never appealed to Meštrović, he was always ready to serve the interests of his country. His patriotism and his reputation as an artist in Western Europe almost immediately propelled him to leadership.

The seat of the four-year activity of this committee was London. Meštrović's personal reputation in England had been well established before he arrived in the spring of 1915. Several of his pieces had been shown in the large Austrian Exhibition held at Earl's Court, London, in 1906. James Bone's articles in the *Manchester Guardian*, first a review of the Rome Exhibition hailing Meštrović as the "New Master" (June 20, 1911), and a second featuring the Kossovo project as a "Serbian Prophecy" (October 31, 1912), gave the artist considerable prestige. Several other reviews had appeared in *The Studio* and *The Art News*. In 1913 he had also visited London for a short time to see the Elgin Marbles in the British Museum.

The beginning of political action of the Yugoslav Committee centered around an exhibit of Meštrović's work organized in London. British friends, aware of the unjust territorial compensations promised Italy in the secret treaty of London (1915), suggested an exhibit to draw the attention of the British public to the cultural achievements of the Yugoslav peoples and to underscore the solidarity of Croats, Serbs, and Slovenes of Austria-Hungary with the Kingdom of Serbia. The impressive result was the famous exhibition in the Victoria and Albert Museum in South Kensington which opened on June 24, 1915. Special guests included Lord Robert Cecil, Undersecretary for Foreign Affairs, representatives of the Yugoslav National Committee and a host of political and social dignitaries. In his opening address Lord Cecil cited the sculpture of Meštrović as a convincing reply to the traditional claim that Germany stood between Europe and the barbarism of the Slavic peoples. "Perhaps this war," he said prophetically "shall some day be looked upon as the beginning of a new influence in Europe, such as has not been seen in the past five centuries."

Reviews by the leading critics, including James Bone, P. G. Konody, John M. Murray, Frank Rutter and C. H. Collins-Baker, repeating what had been expressed in earlier criticism praised the powerful élan, the strong conviction, dynamic form and architectural fitness of his sculpture. The critics also stressed the Kossovo subject matter, particularly the new significance and possibilities under the present conditions of war.

The public reaction, therefore, spread from the interest in the new developments of contemporary sculpture to the cultural and political aspirations of the Yugoslav peoples for national unification and independence. The same exhibition was held in many other cities of the British Isles, including Glasgow and Edinburgh. It stimulated exhibitions of other Serbo-Croatian artists and also provided an opportunity for concerts of Slav music and lectures on southern Slav history, architecture and literature. Meštrović's exhibitions therefore become a major factor in attracting the attention and sympathy of the British public to the national aspirations of the Yugoslav people as expressed through the Yugoslav Committee. They continued through the war and were climaxed in the large exhibition held in Paris at the Petit Palais in 1919 during the time of the Versailles Peace Conference. The frequent reference among later German critics to Meštrović as having served in the *Propagandadienst* of the Serbian government during the war must be understood from this point of view.

The historical tragedy of the Yugoslav situation is the inability of the several races and peoples, whose differences were further intensified by their conflicting church traditions — Roman Catholic in Croatia and Eastern Orthodox in Serbia — to arrive at a common and equitable basis for government. The Yugoslav Committee conceived of the new Yugoslavia as essentially a federation within which the three branches of Serbs, Croats and Slovenes would be equal. The Royal Serbian government saw the future state of the Serbs, Croats and Slovenes as an enlarged Serbia within which the Serbs would play a dominant role.

Although the Yugoslav Committee and the Royal Serbian government worked together for a common goal, the unification of all Serbs, Croats, and Slovenes, they disagreed regarding the internal organization of the future common state. The differences between the Yugoslav Committee and the Serbian government were to a certain extent ironed out by the Corfu Declaration (July 20, 1917) which was to provide the basis for the unification. After the Allied victory in 1918, however, the Serbian army occupied the Yugoslav lands of the disintegrated Austro-Hungarian monarchy. Yugoslav unification was carried out in Belgrade on December 1, 1918 in a manner unacceptable to the Croats and the 1921 centralist Constitution was imposed by the dominant Serbian political parties against the will of a majority of Croats and Slovenes who supported a federal form of government.

During the interwar years most of the ministers, the vast majority of the diplomatic posts, and nearly all the leading military positions were held by Serbs. Meštrović had worked for the establishment of a Yugoslav federation within which the Serbs, Croats and Slovenes would be equal partners and he, as a true patriot, actively opposed Serbian hegemony in the new state. He was alarmed by the bitter Serbo-Croatian conflict and felt that, unless the conflict was settled in a mutually satisfactory manner, it would lead Yugoslavia to disaster. For this reason he repeatedly attempted to bring about a compromise solution which would satisfy the basic and justifiable demands of the Croat people. The result was that his moderate and conciliatory stand subjected him to bitter attack from both Serbian and Croatian extremists.

The record of Meštrović's productivity in sculpture during the war shows many portraits which, with the occasional sale of individual pieces, became his means of livelihood. Part of the time he lived in Geneva where he carved the large wooden crucifix and first panel of the life of Christ series now in his chapel in Split. He also lived for a time in Cannes in southern France. There he did the superb *Archers of Domagoj* which was intended as one of a series similar to the reliefs of the Kossovo project.

Meštrović's major interest however was directed toward religious subjects. The tragedy and suffering of war found release in the *Pietà* and *Madonna and Child* and a number of reliefs depicting scenes from the Life and Passion of Christ. To the heroes of national concern are added the religious parallels in the Old Testament — prophets and leaders, particularly Moses symbolizing the moral authority of the law. His style developed a new phase with a stress on elongated forms related to the movement and design of his own earlier work, but stimulated by medieval Byzantine design. As an influence, this was again thoroughly genuine and personal, since he had known as a boy some of the richest examples of early Christian religious painting on the walls of churches in his native land. The consistent pain and distortion of face and figures provided a new spiritual expression not found in his earlier work. With the release of the end of the war and its tragic pressure he then entered another phase of work in the mature period of the new Yugoslavia.

V

The twenty years between the two wars represented for Europe a period of recovery followed by the economic and political dislocation which threw it back into the same disastrous struggle it had failed to resolve in the first war. For Yugoslavia it was a period of increasing internal strife and tension. The growing Serbo-Croatian conflict affected all aspects of political, economic and cultural life. It absorbed the energies of the people in a barren and ruinous struggle that impeded economic progress, undermined parliamentary government, destroyed civil liberties, and led to police repression and dictatorship. Despite the fact that Meštrović was a leading and influential citizen of the country, the conciliatory role he played in political circles caused him many difficulties. A police agent lived across the street to report on all activities and visitors in the artist's home and, since King Alexander and many Yugoslav ministers as well as foreign diplomats were frequent visitors to his home and studio, this was a constant source of annoyance.

For Meštrović, the sculptor, however, it was a period of integration whereby the various probings and projects of wide diversity were crystalized into mature and permanent monuments. These were largely public in nature, but for the most part they represent his own ideas and purposes with which he had worked from early youth. Some were commissioned and paid for by government or private agencies, such as the monument to *King Peter I* in Dubrovnik, the monument of *Gratitude to France, Tomb of the Unknown Soldier,* and such outside commissions as the Chicago *Indians* and the incompleted *Bolivar* project. Others were his personal gifts to his fellow citizens, monuments to those prophets of the Croatians through whose labors the cultural achievements which form the people's inheritance of the centuries have been preserved, clarified and made available for the benefit of mankind. Thus the great men—Bishop Gregory of Nin, Marko Marulić, Bishop Strossmayer, Petar Berislavić, Andrija Medulić and many others—form a veritable open pantheon of *illustribus viris* distributed among the public squares of his nation's principal cities.

A second area of activity was the architectural projects in the form of churches and memorial chapels which seem to have provided the means for realizing on a more modest scale the Kossovo idea of a national shrine. Perhaps it may be considered a development from the patriotic to the religious, but in the artist's mind the traditional differences between the sacred and secular in artistic expression are less important than their relationship, and his devotion to both has always been direct and complete. It is certain that the war had made a deep impression on him for he well realized its cost in the suffering and destruction of human life, as well as the damage to accumulated cultural heritage. The need for faith and the hope of salvation through Christ's example was apparent in much of the work he did during the war.

In any case, the first major project after his return to Zagreb was the Račić Memorial Church. Ivo Račić was a prominent shipowner whose home was in the village of Cavtat, near Dubrovnik, and whose son and daughter had been living in London during the war when Meštrović made their acquaintance. During the influenza epidemic of 1919, three members of the family died in rapid succession. On her deathbed the daughter, Maria Račić Banac asked her mother, the only surviving member of the family, to have the artist "build me a tomb and console me with the thought that death is but a shadow." As an answer to Maria's request the artist had inscribed on the bronze bell hanging from the cupola: "Know the mystery of love and thou shalt solve the mystery of death and believe that life is eternal."

The following description was given by the eminent scholar and art historian Josef Strzygowski in his introduction to a monograph on the chapel published in 1937 (*Ivan Meštrović: Gospa od Anđelâ*, Zagreb, 1937).

"The memorial church lies on the highest point of a small peninsula. The cemetery with its cypresses occupies the height, and the building rises in its midst. The plan is octagonal, with four projecting chambers along the principal axis: on the east, the vestibule; on the west, the altar-niche; and a chapel to north and south. The central space is crowned by a dome rising in corbelled courses. It ends in a lantern, which rises vertically above the sloping stone roof and culminates in a kneeling bronze angel. The entrance is also flanked by angels which serve as caryatids; and the meaning of the whole building is thereby made plain from the start. The vestibule leads first to a bronze door, whose low reliefs represent the four apostles of the Slavs—SS. Cyril and Methodius, Sava, and Gregory of Nin. The frame is composed of wavy lines, which form circular panels with the four apostles above; and round about, interspersed with other saints, the twelve signs of the Zodiac. Below, under the feet of the lower Apostles, is the symbol of the Serpent.

"On entering the building the visitor, looking through the domed space brightly lit from above, catches a sight of the altar at the end of one arm of the cross and lighted from a window on either side. Two steps lead from the dark pavement up to the altar frontal with the Lamentation over the body of Christ and the Lamb; and from thence to the Mother of God, seated alone before the gabled background, while six naked boy angels make music on either side. Our gaze is directed towards the Mother of God by angels' heads, chiselled in the receding perspective of the coffered ceiling; and by four turned candlesticks on brackets.

"In the main part of the building the pavement is made of five sorts of Dalmatian marble, with severely stylized signs of the planets and symbols of the Evangelists in a circle and octagon about a central star. In the diagonal sides of the octagon are slabs giving access to the crypts; and above these are angels carrying souls in their arms. Still higher, in the dome, angels' heads in small quadrangular recesses, lead up to the bell, which hangs in the open lantern and is of cast bronze, with figures of saints in low relief.

"The lateral arms of the Cross correspond in disposition with the altar-niche, but are more simply arranged. On the end wall to the right is a figure of St. Roch, to the left Christ on the Cross. Let into the side walls are four low reliefs representing the four members of the Račić family to whose memory the building is dedicated.

31

"The building is 16 metres long, 14 metres wide, and 13½ metres high. The exterior is constructed of simple ashlar work. The raking cornices of the transepts and the crowning cornice of the dome are adorned with wavy lines and filling-ornaments of palmettes in the one case and winged lambs between palms in the other. Elsewhere there are antique motifs, with palmettes and the ram's heads."

The first and most remarkable feature of its style is the monumental character of the building itself, crowning as it does the height of the peninsula, enhanced by dark, swaying cypress trees, surrounded by the blue waters of the Adriatic. Its form is the octagonal central building which was also the basic motif of the Kossovo temple. Its interior decoration embodies the strict and elemental restraint of the architecture with its major accents on the Madonna, St. Roch, the Crucifixion and the four intervening angels bearing souls. The reliefs are quite flat so as to retain the clean and solid character of the wall, but the figure design has the elongated expressiveness and movement Meštrović had developed in his religious reliefs of the war period. These, like many of the traditional Christian symbols used in the bronze doors and decorative friezes are related to designs in early Christian churches of Dalmatia but consistently developed in his own way. The tall-proportioned "Madonna and Child" is closely related in its design to the madonna figures done during the war.

The Račić commission placed no restrictions on the manner in which it should be executed so that the artist enjoyed complete freedom of expression. But this was a rare situation as far as religious sculpture is concerned. The poverty of local churches made it impossible for them to purchase sculpture by contemporary artists, so that whatever religious projects Meštrović undertook were given out of his own generosity and common Catholic faith. In a sense this accounts for the freedom and power of his work. Some of these were for existing churches, such as those of St. Mark's Church in Zagreb. Other churches he designed, built and furnished with sculpture at his own expense, a magnificent array of monuments which extends from the first years of his return to Zagreb to the present time: the Meštrović family chapel of the Holy Redeemer in Otavice, the memorial chapel of King Zvonimir in Biskupija, and the cloister and church which he built on his own property in Split with its thirty wood relief panels depicting the life of Christ and a large wooden crucifix.

On his return to Zagreb after the war he refused to serve as a member of the Yugoslav Provisional National Assembly to which he had been chosen. The pressure was strong on him to continue participation in government affairs. At various times he was offered appointments as Senator, Minister of

Education, Croatian member of a three-man regency, and even the position of Prime Minister under King Alexander. He did accept the directorship of the Zagreb Academy of Fine Arts, but he refused all political appointments because he did not agree with the policy of the ruling class in Belgrade.

In 1904 Ivan Meštrović was married to his first wife, Ruža Klein, the Croatian sister-in-law of the Viennese sculptor Josephu. His second marriage took place in 1923 to Olga Kesterčanek, the mother of his four children: Marta (b. 1924), Tvrtko (b. 1925), Marica (b. 1927), and Matthew (b. 1930).

At the time of his second marriage the artist purchased a home in Zagreb, on Mletačka Street, a seventeenth-century mansion which he restored and to which he added an extensive working-studio. It was here that he lived with his family during the winter months until the collapse of Yugoslavia in 1941 and the establishment of the Independent State of Croatia under the aegis of the Axis. At the same time he spent his summers in Split, where, beginning in 1930 he designed and built a substantial home with a magnificent view from its balcony of the surrounding shores and the sea. Many a visitor has commented on this landscape of almost Homeric pathos with its expanse of blue water broken by silver-gray islands worn smooth by the salt and wind of centuries. Their bald, naked and powerful forms, like those of the rugged mountains in the hinterland of his youth were a continuous source of inspiration. These homes in Split and Zagreb are now public museums, the gift of the artist to the Croatian people.

Meštrović's reputation during the period between the wars continued to be international. A first monograph on his ideas and work was published in London in 1919. A second, edited by his close friend Dr. Milan Ćurčin, was published in English, French, German and Serbo-Croatian by the magazine *Nova Evropa* in 1933. There were also countless reviews and articles published in the art periodicals of nearly all European countries. In 1924-25 he spent nine months in the United States with an exhibition of his best work which was shown in the Brooklyn Museum, the Art Institute of Chicago, museums at Detroit and Buffalo, as well as other museums of note. Several pieces were sold, and the monumental equestrian Indian figures in Chicago's Grant Park were commissioned as a result of this visit.

Years of fame and public life had not changed the artist's basic, independent point of view. The story goes that in the original discussion of this latter project it was suggested that he do a figure of an American hero, such as Washington. The response was negative: "That's already been done." "How about Lincoln?" "That's been done too, many times." Agreement was finally reached on the heroic concept of the American Indian which has had its legendary tradition in one way or another since American pioneer days and could be understood as a parallel to both the classic Warrior and the Marko Kraljević myths.

In Europe the French Government through its ministry of education sponsored a large exhibition of his work at the Jeu de Paume in 1933. Subsequently the same group was shown in Prague, Munich, Berlin (in the Reichstag), Vienna and Graz. Already at that time, Meštrović was subjected to the pressure of the new wave of authoritarian nationalism in Germany which was to bring on war and disaster in later years.

Before his assassination in 1934 at Marseilles, King Alexander had commissioned Meštrović to execute the Yugoslav *Tomb of the Unknown Soldier* and the monument to the Montenegrin poet and Prince-Bishop Petar Petrović Njegoš. The latter project was commissioned in 1924 but its execution was postponed at that time because several high-ranking Orthodox clergymen objected to its "non-Byzantine" style. Shortly before the outbreak of the Second World War he was commissioned to carve a monument to the Rumanian statesman, Ion Bratianu for the city of Bucharest (1938) and the following year he completed two large-scale equestrian statues in bronze of King Carol I and King Ferdinand I for Bucharest, both of which were later dismantled and carried off by the Russians when they occupied the city in 1945.

To characterize the evolution of the artist's style in this period as a form of mature classicism is to deny the richness and variety of his accomplishment. To the cultural historian himself the age bracketed by the two world wars defies classification and leaves him only with a host of unsolved problems. Meštrović, motivated from the beginning by great ideas, found himself living in the midst of a situation where these ideals of a people's heritage and destiny were gradually taking realistic form, but whose development was blocked by the lack of the over-all concept under which and through which this integration could take place. Neither church, government, nor society could command the power or appeal to draw the divergent forces of a people together into a common enterprise. Thus the re-achievement of the common faith, which the artist was convinced must have motivated the nameless artisans of the great medieval cathedrals, still remained in the future. Meštrović determined, therefore, to work alone as far as his means and energies would permit, and to prove by demonstration the validity of his ideals.

Great ideas do not develop; they simply *exist*. They exist in all ages and lands, unchanging, eternal. It is the form that changes and develops as man and his creative energies are determined by the available material and conditions of his surroundings. Certainly a classic form is achieved in large projects such as the Račić Memorial, the *Tomb of the Unknown Soldier,* and that of

Njegoš, now in process of completion. But here is a strong tendency to resist the finality of the classic in favor of a spirit more elementary, moving and potentially evolving. Thus Meštrović's interest was continually attracted to the primitive of ancient Greece rather than the Golden Age, the archaic Romanesque and Gothic rather than the Renaissance. As the problems presented their varying requirements, these elements appeared in different degrees of intensity.

One can follow his thinking through a number of comparisons in the illustrations. The cleancut and wonderfully expressive action which appears in the repeated silhouettes of the *Archers of Domagoj* (Fig. 35) receives a quality of hard invincibility in the relief of *The Canadian Phalanx* (Fig. 36), which may well have been determined by the translation from ancient archer to the modern rifle-bearing soldier. The elongated features and linear clarity of earlier portraits and woman figures appear in the decorations of the Račić Memorial and individual figures with musical instruments. Frequent studies of movement in the figure, as the *Girl with Guitar* (Fig. 55), account for the development of the more calm, devotional grace to be found in the beautiful *Madonna and Child* in the Syracuse University collection (Fig. 48). This development can be seen by comparison with the earlier *Madonna* of 1917 (Fig. 29).

Frequently there are direct and realistic studies from nature, such as the portraits of his *Mother in Prayer* and his wife nursing her child, which resolve into the calm dignity of *Croatian History* (Fig. 49) and the rounded forms of the figures in St. Mark's. There is a remarkable series of nude figures in a more classical manner (Fig. 45), not with the compact and forceful realism of the early Kossovo *Widows*, but with the long forms and sharp twisted movement which herald the later *Atlantid* and *Persephone* figures. The concentrated power of the equestrian warrior which he stressed both in the early vase reliefs (Fig. 20) and *Marko Kraljević* appears refined in more archaic terms with the *Shield of Crown Prince Alexander;* and then is developed into the much freer movement and monumental power of the equestrian *Indians* of Chicago. The detail of the model photographed in the artist's studio shows the use of the physical forms, not only the muscular anatomy, but the distorted features of nose, forehead and headdress as expressive masses which carry the total action of the composition.

This is the kind of action which accounts for the remarkable strength of the *Gregory* monument (Fig. 74), set in the center of the peristyle of Diocletian's palace in Split and executed in the same period. Complaints have been many over the years that the towering twenty-six-foot figure was too big and overpowering for the surrounding two-story peristyle. But the distortion was

35

deliberate; this contrast in proportions could not help but enhance the monumental character of the figure. The pose and gesture is a victoriously didactic one. Gregory, Bishop of Nin in the tenth century, opposed Rome in his insistence on the right to read the Mass in Slavonic rather than Latin. He is seen as the leader of the Croats who opposed dictation and so stands as the symbol of victory over ancient imperialism whose ghostly shell was in this century resurrected by renascent Fascism. This symbolic figure was erected in Split in 1929. Small wonder then that the Italian Fascists dismantled the figure and put it in a warehouse when they took over the city in 1941. After the war's end the statue was again erected, but this time outside the Golden Gate of Diocletian's palace, where it remains today as a symbol of Christian will and prophecy.

VI

The outbreak of war in 1941 brought problems and frustrations as disastrous to Meštrović personally as they were to his country. The National-Socialist regime in Germany had paid him considerable attention during the 1930's and these attentions became increasingly obnoxious as the war approached. The monumental form, the power, and vitality of Meštrović's sculpture were attractive to the party élite. He was besieged, therefore, with requests for exhibitions and personal appearances, and in 1935 the Fuehrer informed the Yugoslav ambassador in Berlin that he would personally open Meštrović's exhibition in the Reichstag which was organized by the Prussian Academy, if the artist himself would be there. But the artist replied he could not come to Berlin for the occasion.

After the conquest of Yugoslavia, Hitler and Mussolini established a puppet government in Croatia under the local Quisling, Ante Pavelić. As head of the dread *Ustaša,* a terrorist organization of Croatian nationalists who for years had demanded separation from Yugoslavia, his long and infamous career dated from 1928, when five Croat deputies of the Peasant Party were shot in Parliament by a Montenegrin deputy of the Serbian Radical Party. Stjepan Radić, the Croat Peasant Party leader and two of the other deputies died. The Ustaša organization was set up the next year as a reaction to the continued terrorism and oppression of the Belgrade (Serbian) regime. It was this same Pavelić, a former deputy in the Belgrade parliament who, with the active cooperation of Mussolini and the Italian Fascists, organized the 1934 assassination of King Alexander in Marseilles.

At the very beginning Meštrović greeted the establishment of the Independent State of Croatia with scepticism and rejected all efforts to get him to collaborate with the regime. Within a short time his worst misgivings regarding the independence of Pavelić's Croatia were justified when Pavelić handed to Mussolini a large part of Dalmatian Croatia including Meštrović's native village and the city of Split. The year following Yugoslavia's collapse in 1941 involved not only the seemingly hopeless struggle against the Axis powers, but a fratricidal civil war between the Serbs and Croats which brought destruction to countless villages and death to hundreds of thousands of innocent people.

Meštrović's position, however, was a difficult and desperate one. He was in Split when Yugoslavia was attacked. Early on Easter morning he was awakened by exploding Italian bombs which dropped without warning. After a week the Italian army occupied Split, Meštrović's house was searched for "hidden weapons" and he was subjected to continuous harassment. As usual, he had frequent visitors, including artists and scholars among the officers and enlisted men of the Italian army who were interested in his work. They would come to him individually and as unobtrusively as possible, with a furtive glance over the shoulder to see if they were being watched.

There were repeated requests from German and Italian agencies for his cooperation in the cultural program of the occupying forces. These he stubbornly refused. His friend Giovanni Papini sent him a message through an Italian officer that he should leave Split, because the Fascists had decided to liquidate him. At the same time the commanding Italian general told Bishop Bonifačić of Split, that the Italian government planned to arrest and deport Meštrović to Italy. The Bishop told the general, "Meštrović is only an artist and is highly respected by the people." The general answered, "He shall be the first to be jailed because he was most responsible that Italy did not get Dalmatia after the First World War."

Meštrović also received a phone call from Mile Budak, a well-known Croatian writer and Minister of Education in Pavelić's government. Budak warned the sculptor of his impending arrest by the Italian Fascists and urged him to come to Zagreb. Thereupon Meštrović left for Zagreb where Budak tried to help him obtain a passport and the necessary visas to go abroad. But after ten days the Ustaša police arrested Meštrović and took him to the Savska Cesta prison. It so happened that General von Glaise-Horstenau, an Austrian with the German army, came to call on the sculptor that very day and on learning of his arrest informed the Ustaša authorities that he would hold them responsible for Meštrović's life. Thus it was that the "accidental" murder of the artist was prevented.

The sculptor remained in prison for four and a half months. It is perhaps pointless to repeat the story he told of the long days and endless nights listening to the psychotic yelling, talking, arguing of fanatics in the halls outside his cell. Names were called in the middle of the night and men were led away never to be seen again. It was an increasingly degrading spectacle of people without honor or self-respect, who would turn against their own mothers, wives and sisters, if there was any advantage to be gained for themselves. Their one fear was for their own lives. Out of this misery Meštrović found pity for them and inner peace.

After months of negotiating by friends through the Vatican, Meštrović was released for the purpose of executing a number of commissions in Rome. He lived there for several months, and it was during this interlude that he did a bust of *Pope Pius XII*, several pieces for the Croatian Institute of St. Jerome, the gigantic *Pietà,* and an over life-size relief of *The Stigmata of St. Francis* for the church of St. Mary the Mediator in Rome. The three years following he lived in Switzerland with his wife and four children first in Lausanne, later in Geneva.

The years in Switzerland were difficult ones. Not only was he hampered by lack of working facilities, but he became desperately ill with phlebitis for several months in 1945, and the long hoped-for return to a peaceful Yugoslavia became thwarted by the success of the Communists. In 1946 he returned to Rome where he completed some of the works exhibited in the year following at the Metropolitan Museum in New York. From that time on, there were many offers and invitations by the Communist government for Meštrović to return and take up his work where he left it in 1941. But developments in Yugoslavia did not inspire his sympathy or confidence. The memory of the prison cell was too fresh, the record of the Communist policy toward the Church and the rights of the individual was too vivid, and the new religion of totalitarian materialism was all too obvious for him to surrender to its embrace. From Tito himself came the offer of complete personal freedom and material wealth. His property—studios, home and other real estate—had never been confiscated and were waiting there for him to return, but he steadfastly refused to go back in protest against the government's abuse of the rights and liberties of his countrymen. He could not live in abundance and personal freedom when others were poverty-stricken and deprived of their liberty.

It was at this juncture that the offer of a professorship at Syracuse University was made by Chancellor William P. Tolley who heard of his plight through Malvina Hoffman, well-known American sculptress and author. It was a major decision for the artist which meant the beginning of a new life with new vistas and an ever broadening horizon. Its orientation, as will be seen, remained fixed on the same basic objectives he had maintained from his early youth.

The prison cell of Savska Cesta, however, was the real turning point toward a new style and development which was revealed full-blown in the impressive one-man show held at the Metropolitan Museum in New York in 1947. Alternate and confused feelings of helpless resentment, loneliness, hope and resignation—"nothing to do but sit and think," he said simply— brought literally torrents of ideas, yet utter frustration through lack of means by which to express them. The best he could do was a series of drawings.

The fateful turmoil of resentment, compassion and faith at this time was for him no longer the poetic expression of a people's history but a deep personal experience. "Behold, I cry out of wrong, but I am not heard. . . ." (Job: 19,7); the sufferings of Job had a very real meaning to him; it was no accident that one of the most significant works which developed out of this period was the powerful figure of *Job* in the Syracuse University collection. But the artistic release appeared in several ways and a new religious character can be followed through a number of particular themes, notably the studies of prophets, *St. Francis,* the suffering of the *Pietà* and particularly the *Women under the Cross.*

It will be remembered that one of the distinguishing features of Meštrović's portraits was his emphasis on character expression. His interest in the strong and dedicated characters whom he saw as prophets of his people is evident in his selection of personalities for public monuments, most of which were his personal gifts. There were several figures of evangelists, such as *Luke* and *John* in 1929, shown as inspired instruments of God. A strong and aggressive monumental head of *Moses* appeared as a parallel to the mighty *Gregory of Nin* in 1926.

The ideas for *Jerome* and *Job* appear in drawings done in the prison cell. St. Jerome had actively taught in Dalmatia and had been claimed by the Croatians since the early Middle Ages as their patron saint. Meštrović's first commission, when he arrived in Rome, was the powerfully Michelangelesque relief of this scholar-saint for the Croatian Institute, along with the parallel portrait of the Croatian *Pope Sixtus V.*

A companion piece to the *St. Jerome,* this is intended as a tribute to the great sixteenth-century reformer and builder, who completed the dome of St. Peter's, expanded the Vatican library and rebuilt the Lateran Palace, as well as zealously supporting the Counter-reformation movement. Pope Sixtus V (1585-90) was of Croatian descent, and had been Bishop, then Cardinal-priest of St. Jerome of the Slavs, before his ascension to the papacy.

Significant is the development of the seated figure and scholarly gesture from the Roman relief of St. Jerome to the bronze three-dimensional composition of the same saint in which the figure squats Gandhi-like with knees thrust outward, head sunk deep in spiritual contemplation. Meštrović's interpretation of its meaning is given in his own painting of St. Jerome in the same pose with visions of the Crucified Christ, an angel playing a musical instrument and the Egyptian god Horus floating above him.

The anguished and protesting cry of the Old Testament *Job* is a didactic parallel to the philosophic resignation and peace of *Jerome*. The same pose is used, with tensely cramped hands and head turned sharply upward. It is a more actively open composition than the restfully closed one of the *Jerome*. Here too the related painting of the *Argument of Job* suggests the questioning disputation so characteristic of the Biblical text.

Meštrović did many figures of Christ on the Cross and Crucifixion scenes through his career, including a drawing at this time. But what attracted him here were the more direct and penetrating details or variations which give that Sacrifice its significance to the individual. From the inexhaustible repertory of Christian iconography he chose those subjects which have personal significance: thus, the *Stigmata of St. Francis* rather than the intently praying saint of many years ago (Fig. 94). There is a considerable number of weeping, sorrowful women, particularly *Mary Magdalene under the Cross*. They look upward with varied expressions of anguish and hope, sometimes with the impulsive gesture of upstretched arms characteristic of the traditional Magdalene.

These gestures have meaning in terms of expressive form. Like the muscular tension limited to the torso of *Strahinja Ban,* the spiritual tension of anguished prayer appears in a seated *Magdalene* used as a single relief figure as far back as 1919 (Fig. 31). They appear in a drawing (1941) of the *Noli Me Tangere* (Fig. 77) and in the several Crucifixion scenes. Indeed they furnish the clue to the more Christian interpretation which Meštrović gave to the classic Venus figure.

Supplicant Persephone (Fig. 96) and the *Atlantid* are basically full-figure studies of the female form which he had used before in the Kossovo *Widows* and the various reclining or standing figures done in the middle twenties: *Woman by the Sea* (Fig. 42); *Dreaming* (Fig. 44); and especially *Psyche* (Fig. 45). Where the *Widows* had the uncomfortable twist of his youthful realism, the *Psyche* has the more formal and refined movement of Michelangelo's figures. With *Persephone* the movement is extended beyond the figure with its upswept arms, cramped hands and twisted head and neck in its Magdalenian expression of suffering and prayer. The prefix "supplicant" which the artist added to the usual title suggests that interpretation to the mythical goddess doomed to the dark realm of Pluto but striving for liberation. Hence the figure stands as a dramatic symbol of the suffering of the human soul.

Anguish in other terms is given in the parallel *Atlantid* whereby the movement is held within itself and, through its serpentine gestures, to the space around the figure. This theme is taken up in a new variation in *Supplication* (Fig. 97) where the crouched figure of Job is clothed and developed in a strong and compact expression through the gesture, drapery and upturned head.

It is suggested earlier that Meštrović's introduction to sculpture had been through the medium of the stone mason and the form of Rodin and Michelangelo. Rodin was more immediate, but Michelangelo hovered in the future as an ideal. Years in Rome, but particularly the crucial experience of 1941-42, brought a new insight into the unique character of piety and power represented in the work of the great Florentine. Probably the most significant work to come out of this combination of circumstances, and indeed the artist's most monumental accomplishment of the Second War period, is the giant *Pietà*. It began with a small drawing in the Zagreb prison, was modeled in Rome after his release and was completed during a short visit to Rome in 1946. The twelve-foot, five-and-a-half ton Carrara marble piece was first shown in the great Metropolitan exhibition in New York and is now located in Sacred Heart Church on the campus of Notre Dame University in South Bend, Indiana.

VII

A major principle to be understood in the character and development of that enigmatic phenomenon called "American" is the constant flow of European artists and intellectuals who for generations have fled tyranny and oppression in their homeland and found a new freedom and opportunity in the New World. By tradition they have brought knowledge and skills, but what has been far more significant, they have also brought maturity and a sense of spiritual values which have played no small part in establishing the cultural equilibrium necessary to the survival of a great and free nation.

The impact of Meštrović, particularly as he appeared through the great Metropolitan Museum exhibition in 1947, demonstrated again the significance of this tradition. It had no political overtones, as was the case in the

41

important exhibitions of earlier times in the Vienna Secession, the 1911 Rome International, the London show of 1915, or the Paris exhibition of 1919. In the Metropolitan show he was presented as an artist and humanitarian who was able to speak simply and directly through the medium of stone, wood and bronze.

With a long record of exhibitions in America as well as in Europe, and the many publications of his work, Meštrović was well known. But he had been forgotten during the interval of the war and contemporary sculpture had developed along other lines than the one he had followed for nearly five decades. He once said jokingly that his trouble was that he did not die soon enough, but in the same breath, he added he was very grateful because there was still much work to be done. This remark came shortly before his seventy-fifth birthday when he was continuing on a ten-hour daily work schedule.

The reaction in the press to the Metropolitan exhibition was almost universally genuine and enthusiastic. The qualifying "almost" is added because controversy has always been an important ingredient in contemporary American art criticism, and there were indeed complaints about Meštrović as a foreigner and a conservative. "Meštrović retains much of his earlier power and strength...," said Carlyle Burrows in the *Christian Science Monitor* of April 26, 1947. He pointed out his large sense of form and his evident ability to interpret that form with power in heroic concepts. "Most impressive," Burrows wrote, "is the figure of *Job* on which Meštrović has lavished emotional force beyond any of his other works, achieving with realism a prodigious sense of the subject's spiritual and physical torment."

In the *New York Times* (April 11, 1947) Edward Alden Jewell featured the retrospective character of the show and an analysis of its stylistic derivations. There were Classic and Renaissance phases as well as Archaic and Naturalistic, the critic recognized, "but the work . . . certainly leaves in no doubt his power and originality; the thoroughness with which influences have been assimilated. . . ." In commenting on the classical feeling of the *Persephone* and *Atlantid,* he insisted that ". . . This is no mere classicism of the academies. The figures are characterized by a kind of disciplined violence . . . seeming to reflect something generic in the sculptor's native environment" which he considered especially eloquent and original.

Margaret Cresson, also in the *New York Times* (April 6, 1947) spoke of him as the "sculptor's sculptor," whose work, though thoroughly grounded in anatomy, could never be called academic because it was too original and too universal. His is a classical balance between vigor, even violence, and dignity. He is modern in that his work is fresh and does not fall into categories. But he is no "modernist" in that he never strives after effects for their own sake.

42

In commenting on a show at the Boston Museum School several years later, Dorothy Adlow in the *Christian Science Monitor* for March 9, 1951, quoted Meštrović's advice that "everyone should be sincere with himself and the world, find his own best medium, realize his own capacity and do what he must do." What impressed her was the artist's striving for simplicity and dignity, his respect for the archaic styles rather than the Renaissance, the primitive Greek rather than that of the Golden Age. "This sculptor" she concluded, "brings to his works the knowledge of a lifetime and to his subject a personal understanding of vicissitudes and pathos."

These comments have to do with the sculptor as an artist, not a patriot. To a younger generation, going through adolescent growing pains toward new forms of artistic expression, the impact of Meštrović's work was one of maturity and confidence based on personal achievement. To him, art and spiritual content are not to be separated, but to his new American audience the initial point of contact seemed to be through the pure medium of form. As time went on and the warm glow of World War victory faded into a new set of international tensions, the interest of the public gradually shifted toward the larger problems of human rights. In this connection this particular artist's personal struggle to maintain a universal faith as reflected in his work took on new significance.

The incredibly inspiring and meaningful story of his achievement in the succeeding decade is quickly told. His carriage-house studio on the campus of Syracuse University became the lively center of many activities as had been customary in former years in Zagreb and Split. Graduate students were attracted there from all parts of the country to study with "The Professor" as he was called. Churchmen, educators, museum directors, architects and European compatriots came to him, not only because of his well-deserved reputation for congenial hospitality, but because of some project or enterprise they wanted him to undertake. In a sense this is in the American tradition and is the reason for so many frustrations on the part of artists whose reputations make them public property to the detriment of both artist and prospective patron.

But the list of works produced is impressive. Some of them were doomed to failure, like the gigantic monument to the six million Jews lost through Nazi oppression destined for Riverside Drive in New York City. A fund campaign had been established, much planning and actual working models created, even to the three times life-size figures of Moses and migrating peoples, but in the end the project was lost in the labyrinth of committees.

On the other hand, new and successful projects were accomplished in many different parts of the country: a St. Andrew for an Episcopal church

43

dedicated to that saint in Honolulu, Hawaii, a twenty-four-foot bronze figure for the new Mayo Clinic in Rochester, Minnesota, a Crucifixion for Trinity Lutheran church, also in Rochester, a St. Antony for the College of St. Antony in Oxford, England, decorations for the new nurses' building in Bellevue Hospital in New York, Commissions for Notre Dame University, the National Shrine of the Immaculate Conception in Washington, two monuments in Florida and a number of Catholic commissions which are among the most important of our time. There were likewise many portrait commissions. This was all new work and did not include the expression of interest reflected in the acquisition of individual pieces by museums throughout the country.

Viewed in historical perspective, this presents another phenomenon. As noted earlier in the brief review of art in Europe from 1900 to the beginning of the First World War, there was an amazing amount of activity in the creative arts—new ideas, new forms, and above all, a reasonably stable and consistent patronage to support them. This was true of America as much as it was of Europe. But nearly two generations of war, depression, nationalism, industrialization, government patronage and the lack of it, have mechanized artistic effort, so that the genuinely creative and progressive artist has been obliged to retreat from the market place and go it alone as best he can. The profitable areas of the market place for the sculptors—portraiture, religious art, public monuments and architectural decoration—have been left to the academic and incompetent and hence have almost deteriorated to the point of nonexistence.

The period after the Second World War in America saw the rise of a new generation of sculptors whose inventiveness and productivity carry the promise of a renaissance unheard of in contemporary art. It was sparked by the new architecture, whose clean structure, free movement and open interwoven spaces seem to demand the traditional collaboration of sculptor and architect to give them human meaning.

In this, Meštrović the "conservative" has become the pioneer of a new era. Yet he has fought these battles before. Indeed, it is he who seems to bridge the gap between the progressive art of the early century and that of its third quarter, the open periods bounding the two wars rather than the closed and uneasy one between them.

The possibilities are unlimited. If one were to review any of the major projects to which sculptors have been assigned in the past: the portraits of our illustrious men and women, monuments which express and reflect the collective aspirations of our society, the embellishment of our public places of worship with inspired works of art, and the sculptural enrichment of architecture in general, we would be hard pressed to find anything of quality in the mid-twentieth century beyond the cold tomb of a Jefferson and the banal defacement of a Mount Rushmore.

That the sculptured monuments of the late 1890's and early 1900's were so bad was not the fault of the people, or the government or the church, but directly the responsibility of the artist. It was in this situation that the stubborn young Croatian peasant was unique — the "phenomenon" as Rodin called him. He arrived on the scene fired with an idea and in a remarkably short time had developed the means of expressing it. But he was poor, a peasant, a Croatian, and therefore the underdog; while gigantic sculptural monstrosities honoring emperors, national unities and their worldly conquests went up in every capital, the Kossovo Temple was never built.

This is by no means to say that Meštrović, the prophet, has gone without honor, either in his own country or abroad. On the contrary, few contemporaries have received such universal acclaim as creative artist and humanist. Though well beyond the usual academic retirement age, universities were bidding for his services both as sculptor and teacher, which accounts for his leaving Syracuse University to accept an appointment at the University of Notre Dame in 1955. A half dozen monographs on his work have been published in several languages. The bibliography of articles, criticisms and news items about him and his work runs into the thousands. Honorary degrees have been accorded the artist by Columbia, Colgate, Notre Dame, Marquette and many other colleges and universities. Awards of merit have been presented to him by the American Academy of Arts and Letters and the American Institute of Architects. He is a Grand Officer of the *Legion d'Honeur* and an honorary member of art academies in various European cities. In Yugoslavia today he is considered almost a deity; his works are recognized and exhibited as one of the world's greatest artists and are featured in nearly every publication dealing with cultural affairs. He continues to exhibit his sculpture in Europe and America, and with each exhibit goes the idea which he has believed in and fostered from his earliest youth.

This "idea" has for Meštrović many facets. "One must be in love with eternity," he wrote in his comments on Michelangelo published in *Nova Evropa* in 1926, "so that one's works are at least a shadow of it. . . . Immortality lies imprisoned within us. We must release it to the light. . . . It is written that the Word was from the beginning and that it came from God. But it is not revealed whether the Word was first spoken or carved."

Meštrović is something of a mystic, but he is also a realist in his almost brutal directness in handling material and fact. Again in speaking of Michelangelo in the same essay, he refers to that other "eye." "That other eye . . . the

45

eye of the soul . . . is much more important (and plays a far greater role) than the body's eye, both in the conception of sculpture and in its execution. For example, even before the sculptor lays his chisel to the rough stone (or wood or other material in front of him) he sees within it the figure he wishes to make, even though the block's shape has no resemblance to his envisaged work. He sees the figure not only in rough outline but precisely and in detail from all sides. Logically this means that the creation is already completed, in its total harmony, without the hand or the eye taking part. All that remains for the sculptor is to draw the statue out of the material and reveal it to the physical eye."

In reviewing the published documents over the years, this basic concept has not changed. Referring to his London exhibition and the Kossovo fragments in 1915, this idea of the inner eye is associated with the *guslar:* "The priest of the Temple is the blind wanderer who goes over the earth looking for the Eternal Empire and, looking there, he sees that all men are brothers, all truths are only part of one great truth, all churches only flames which burn to the glory of one Eternal Light, Who lit them all and Who shines through them all."

This inner vision was the element which he sought to dramatize in the many versions of the blind Homer (Fig. 179). It strengthened his sympathy for younger artists whose concern with form appears to be limited to their own personal expression and individual "slice of life." Perhaps some day they will comprehend the larger problems of people, nations and humanity.

It is an inner vision, but it also involves faith and compassion. In 1945 he published a Christmas dialogue based on a drawing representing the Virgin and Child, with music-making angels and the traditional *Badnjak* or Yule log. This he had done on wrapping paper when in prison and sent to his family as a Christmas greeting. The little book is the spiritual journal of a dedicated artist, full of human sympathy and understanding, yet direct and uncompromising in his judgment of problems dealing with art, politics, ethics, economics and religion.

Dennoch Will Ich Hoffen, it is called, for like Job Meštrović still had faith. This was written during the war, when the Italians in Split had pulled down his *Gregory of Nin;* the Serbs had destroyed his *Christ and the Madonna* in the memorial church of King Zvonimir; and his own countrymen, the "liberators" of Croatia, had put him in jail with Jews and other "criminals." Even after the war, the Russian liberators of Bucharest pulled down his heroic equestrian statues of Rumanian *King Carol I, King Ferdinand I* and the statesman *Ion Bratianu* and carried them off as trophies to the U.S.S.R.

46

What Meštrović has frequently said of Michelangelo is equally true of himself. An artist's environment, he insists, is not a determining influence. On the contrary, the inner man is independent and has the right and duty to cling to his own values. Such defiance begets that other and superior kind of hero, like St. Francis and Michelangelo. "We do not separate ourselves from the rest of humanity so that faith in ourselves means faith in mankind."

Thus it is that Meštrović has continued to fight his battle for human rights, freedom and the dignity of man. Certainly he has raised his voice with everyone else against individual injustice, as in the case of Cardinal Stepinac. But the real battle is waged with his own weapons. In 1954 he completed a series of thirty large wooden reliefs depicting the Life of Christ, involving endless years of work, and sent them to Yugoslavia for installation in his chapel in Split as his gift to his countrymen. Similarly the monuments to *Petar Njegoš, Mila Gojsalić, Andrija Kačić Miošić, John the Baptist, St. Antony* and others have been sent as gifts of the artist to his people as reminders of great men and the great ideas by which they lived. Though the ruling group may look upon religion as legendary superstition and history as a reflection of contemporary ideology, those in political power cannot control the vitality of a true work of art. These monuments will eternally serve, embody and actively nourish the latent spirit of freedom which continues to glow behind grim curtains of silence.

Chronology

1883

August 15, born in Vrpolje in the Sava valley of Croatia. Childhood passed with his family in the small mountain village of Otavice in Dalmatian Croatia.

1898

Apprenticed to the stonecutter, Pavle Bilinić, in Split.

1899

Studied in Vienna with Otto Koenig, retired professor, in preparation for entering the Academy.

1900

Accepted by the Academy of Art in Vienna; spent four years working in sculpture under Edmund Hellmer, Hans Bitterlich, Otto Wagner, and others.

1902

Work exhibited in the annual student show of the Academy attracted the attention of the Vienna Secession group.

1903

Became a regular exhibiting member of the Vienna Secession group.

1904

Married Ruža Klein. Bronze fountain, *At the Well of Life,* exhibited in the Secession and purchased by Karl Wittgenstein, whose additional purchases made possible a two-month tour of Italy and subsequent removal to Paris.

1905-1907

First work exhibited in Paris (Salon d'Automne) attracted the attention of Auguste Rodin. First designs for Kossovo monument developed while resident in Paris.

1909

First major exhibition at Vienna Secession, over fifty pieces, the majority of which were connected with the Kossovo monument. Pieces chosen for purchase for the Belvedere collection were rejected by order of the Archduke Franz Ferdinand.

1910

Second major exhibition held in Zagreb, capital of Croatia.

1911

Exhibition of over seventy pieces in the Serbian Pavilion of the International

Exhibition in Rome marked Meštrović as an internationally important sculptor, as well as a factor in the Serbo-Croatian national movement.

1914

Forced to flee from Split at the outbreak of war, following the assassination of Archduke Franz Ferdinand. Lived and worked in Rome as a political exile.

1914-1915

Served in London as an active member of the Yugoslav Committee on national independence.

1915

Major exhibition of work shown in the Victoria and Albert Museum, London, then subsequently in Edinburgh, Glasgow and other cities in the British Isles.

1916-1918

Exile continued in Geneva and Cannes.

1919

Returned to Zagreb. Member of the Yugoslav Provisional National Assembly for a short time only. Resigned and refused further political office.

1919

Exhibition of sculpture held at Petit Palais in Paris coincidental with the Versailles Peace Conference. First monograph, *Ivan Meštrović*, edited by Dr. Milan Ćurčin, published in London.

1919-1922

Designed and executed the large memorial Chapel for the Račić family in Cavtat.

1923

Married Olga Kesterčanek. Purchased and restored seventeenth-century home in Zagreb, now a public gallery devoted to his work.

1924-1925

Nine-month visit to the United States and series of exhibitions in New York (Brooklyn Museum), Chicago (Art Institute), Detroit, Buffalo and other cities.

1925

Commission for two equestrian *Indians* for Grant Park, Chicago.

1926

Execution of monument of *Gregory, Bishop of Nin*, the gift of Meštrović to the city of Split.

1930

Designed and built large summer home at Split, which, with many sculptures and drawings, was donated by the artist to the Croatian people following the Second World War. It is now a public gallery.

1933

One-man exhibition in Paris arranged by the French government in the Jeu de Paume. This exhibit subsequently toured Prague, Berlin, Munich, Vienna and Graz.

1933

Second monograph published in Zagreb, Dr. Milan Ćurčin, editor.

1934

Commissioned by King Alexander I to execute the Yugoslav monument to the *Unknown Soldier* on Mount Avala near Belgrade.

1936

Erected large family chapel in his native village of Otavice.

1937

Designed and built memorial chapel to the medieval Croat *King Zvonimir* near Knin in Croatia.

1938

Designed church with cloister on his own property in Split to house Crucifix and series of thirty wood panel reliefs depicting scenes from the life of Christ. This church was given by the artist to the Croatian people as a place of worship.

1938

Executed heroic granite statue of Rumanian statesman *Ion Bratianu* for the city of Bucharest.

1938-1939

Executed over life-size equestrian figure of Rumanian *King Carol I* and monument (33 feet) of *King Ferdinand I.*

1941

Arrested in Zagreb; imprisoned four and one-half months by local gestapo of the puppet government established by Hitler and Mussolini.

1942

Released from prison; allowed to leave the country; worked in Rome on various commissions for the Vatican; executed a bust of *Pope Pius XII*, a figure of *St. Jerome*, the large *Pietà* and an over life-size relief, *The Stigmata of St. Francis*, for the church of St. Mary Mediator.

1943-1946

Lived and worked in Lausanne and Geneva; seriously ill at Geneva in 1945.

1946

Accepted call to Syracuse University, Syracuse, New York, as Professor of Sculpture in the School of Art.

1947

Exhibition of twenty-five pieces at the Metropolitan Museum of New York under the joint sponsorship of the Museum and the American Academy of Arts and Letters. This is the first time in the Museum's history of seventy-five years that a living artist was honored with a one-man show.

1948

Was awarded honorary degrees by Colgate and Ohio Wesleyan Universities. Publication of monograph, *The Sculpture of Ivan Meštrović*, Syracuse University Press.

1952

Elected honorary member of the Vienna Academy of Fine Arts.

1953

Presented Award of Merit by the American Academy of Arts and Letters of which he was already an honorary member (1947).

1954

Became a citizen of the United States.

1954

Executed fourteen-foot seated figure of *Petar Petrović Njegoš*, poet and Prince Bishop of Montenegro. This figure was donated to the people of Montenegro and erected on Mount Lovčen in 1958.

1955

Awarded the Fine Arts Medal for outstanding achievement in the field of architectural decoration by the American Institute of Architects. Awarded honorary degrees by Marquette University and the University of Notre Dame.

1955

Called to the University of Notre Dame, South Bend, Indiana, as Professor of Sculpture.

List of Illustrations

1. *At the Well of Life*
Fountain, bronze, life-size, 1904. Theater Square, Zagreb, with the National Theater in the background.

2. *At the Well of Life*

3. *At the Source of Life*
Fountain, black granite, 1904-6. Palais Wittgenstein, Vienna.

4. *Tolstoi*
Bronze, under life-size, 1902. Meštrović Gallery, Split, Dalmatia.

5. *The Kossovo Temple*
Model in wood, 1912. State Museum, Belgrade.

6. *Marko Kraljević*
Plaster, study, 1910. State Museum, Belgrade.

7. *Marko Kraljević*
Plaster, study of head, over life-size, 1910. State Museum, Belgrade.

8. *Banović Strahinja*
Marble, over life-size, 1907. Victoria and Albert Museum, London. A plaster pre-liminary sketch of this torso exists in the State Museum at Belgrade. The marble piece itself was presented to the Victoria and Albert Museum at the conclusion of the great exhibition of Meštrović's work there in 1915 as his token of appreciation for the sympathy and understanding shown by the British people for the Yugoslav cause.

9. *Srdja Zlopogledja*
Plaster, twice life-size, 1908. State Museum, Belgrade. This figure was particularly popular in the 1915 London exhibition and details of the head especially were used for both posters and catalogue covers.

10. *The Maiden of Kossovo*
Marble, life-size, 1907. State Museum, Belgrade. Based on the ballad of the same name which glorifies the legendary Maiden who cared for the wounded heroes on the battlefield of Kossovo.

11. *Widows*
Marble, over life-size, 1907. State Museum, Belgrade.

12. *Memories*
Detail of head (Fig. 13).

13. Memories
Marble, over life-size, 1907. State Museum, Belgrade.

14. Widow
Marble, over life-size, 1907. State Museum, Belgrade.

15. Widow
Detail of head (Fig. 14).

16. Widow with Child
Plaster, over life-size, 1912. State Museum, Belgrade.

17. Caryatids and Sphinx
Plaster, over life-size, 1907-8. State Museum, Belgrade. This illustration is from a restoration of an old, damaged photograph, taken at the 1909 Vienna Secession exhibition, giving the general scheme of the entrance corridor through the atrium into the great central hall. The same plan was used in the Serbian Pavilion in the International Exposition in Rome in 1911.

18. Caryatid
Walnut, over life-size, 1911. State Museum, Belgrade.

19. Vase with Frieze of Dancers
Bronze, 4 ft. high, 1908. Originally part of the Wittgenstein collection. One of several vases executed in bronze or stone during the Paris period. This one is significant through its use of the long-necked, attenuated shape of the vase, characteristic of Secession and Art Nouveau design and the expressively elongated figures, related to Egyptian Eighteenth Dynasty reliefs.

20. Vase with Frieze of Warriors
Marble, 3 ft. high, 1909.

21. Vase with Frieze of Warriors and Peasants
Marble, 3 ft. high, 1909.

22. My Mother
Marble, life-size, 1908. State Museum, Belgrade. The first of several versions executed in Split after his return from Paris where he had been working on the Kossovo project. Clothed in the typical costume of the artist's native province the figure is significant as a character portrait related to the various Motherhood and Croatian national themes. A variation of this figure is in the collection of the Art Institute of Chicago.

23. My Father
Bronze, life-size, 1910. State Museum, Belgrade.

24. Portrait of the Artist's Mother
Bronze, life-size, 1909. Meštrović Gallery, Split, Dalmatia.

25. Portrait of Auguste Rodin
Plaster, life-size, 1914. Meštrović Museum, Zagreb.

26. The Victor
Bronze, 16 ft. high, 1913. Belgrade. Monument erected in Kalemegdan Park in Belgrade to commemorate the Serbian victory of 1912 over the Turks in the Battle of Kumanovo.

27. Portrait of Lady Ratcliffe
Bronze, life-size, 1917. Ratcliffe Collection, Leeds, England.

28. Archangel Gabriel
Marble, over life-size, 1919. Brooklyn Museum, New York.

29. Madonna and Child
Walnut, life-size, 1917. Collection of the artist, South Bend, Indiana.

30. Angel
Walnut, life-size, 1917. Ratcliffe Collection, Leeds, England.

31. *Mary Magdalene under the Cross*

Marble, life-size, 1919. Collection of the Masaryk Family, Prague.

32. *Christ on the Cross*

Plaster, life-size, 1914. Meštrović Museum, Zagreb.

33. *Moses*

Drawing, conte crayon, 1916. Meštrović Museum, Zagreb.

34. *Moses*

Plaster, under life-size, 1915. Meštrović Museum, Zagreb.

35. *The Archers of Domagoj*

Plaster, life-size, 1917. Collection of Dr. R. W. Seton-Watson, London.

36. *The Canadian Phalanx 1914-1918*

Marble, 1918. Ottawa, Ontario. Relief executed in Rome at the request of the Canadian War Memorials Commission.

37. *Portrait of the Artist's Wife and Child*

Bronze, 1924. Czechoslovak Modern Gallery, Prague.

38. *Mother and Child*

Marble, life-size, 1922. Fine Arts Gallery, San Diego, California.

39. *My Mother*

Marble, under life-size, 1926. Art Institute, Chicago. One of several variations of which this is probably the most impressive. Other versions are to be found in the Meštrović Gallery in Zagreb and the Jeu de Paume in Paris.

40. *My Mother at Prayer*

Marble, over life-size, 1926. Toronto Art Gallery, Toronto, Ontario.

41. *Mother's Offering*

Marble, over life-size, 1927. Meštrović Gallery, Split, Dalmatia.

42. *Woman by the Sea*

Marble, over life-size, 1926. Meštrović Gallery, Split, Dalmatia.

43. *Woman Reposing*

Marble, over life-size, 1925. Meštrović Museum, Zagreb.

44. *Dreaming*

Marble, over life-size, 1927. Meštrović Gallery, Split, Dalmatia.

45. *Psyche*

Marble, over life-size, 1927. Meštrović Museum, Split, Dalmatia.

46. *Woman with a Harp*

Marble relief, over life-size, 1930. Meštrović Gallery, Split, Dalmatia. A bronze cast of this relief was purchased by the French government for its Jeu de Paume collection after the artist's exhibition in Paris in 1933.

47. *Woman with Guitar*

Bronze, life-size, 1929. Meštrović Gallery, Split, Dalmatia.

48. *Madonna and Child*

Diorite, life-size, 1928. Collection of Syracuse University, Syracuse, New York.

49. *Croatian History*

Marble, over life-size, 1932. State Museum, Belgrade. Stone slab on the figure's lap bears the title "History of Croatia" in Glagolitic script, the Slavonic alphabet in which the early liturgy is written and which is still used by the Croatian Roman Catholic churches by special license of the Pope. The figure was originally intended for the entrance hall of the proposed Museum of Croatian Antiquities at Knin; later bought by King Alexander I for his palace at Dedinje.

50. Console Figure

Walnut (detail of head, Fig. 52). Though the large forms and muscular development of these two figures show strong Michelangelesque characteristics, a closer view reveals the clean, angular and extended forms which give a spiritual and expressive quality related to the period of the First World War.

51. Console Figure

Walnut, over life-size, 1929. Collection of the artist, South Bend, Indiana.

52. Console Figure

Walnut, over life-size, 1929. Collection of the artist, South Bend, Indiana.

53. Adam

Walnut, over life-size, 11 ft. 5 in. high, 1939. Meštrović Gallery, Split, Dalmatia. Executed in Split along with the companion *Eve*, just before the Second World War and related to the male console and caryatid figures.

54. Eve

Walnut, 11 ft. 5 in. high, 1939. Meštrović Gallery, Split, Dalmatia.

55. Girl with Guitar

Black marble, life-size, 1927. Tate Gallery, London.

56. Marko Marulić

Bronze, over life-size, 1925. Meštrović Gallery, Zagreb. One of several head variations of the *Marulić* monument in Split.

57. Marko Marulić

Bronze, over life-size, 1924. Split, Dalmatia. Marko Marulić (1450-1524) was a major interest of Meštrović during his early days in Vienna. This full-length monument was presented by the artist to the town of Split when the artist was home to commemorate the 400th anniversary of the hero's death.

58. Indian with Spear

Plaster, over life-size, 1926. Meštrović Museum, Zagreb. One of the full-scale models for the Chicago project photographed in the artist's Zagreb studio in 1927. Though based on anatomical structure, the figure displays something of the expressive power achieved through distortion.

59. Indian with Bow

Bronze, over life-size, 1926-27. Grant Park, Chicago. Commissioned shortly after the opening of the artist's Chicago exhibition and completed in his Zagreb studio. Though built as three-dimensional forms (see Fig. 58) they are designed essentially as reliefs, since their monumental effect is as silhouettes against the sky when one approaches from either side.

60. Indian with Spear

Bronze, over life-size, 1926-27. Grant Park, Chicago.

61. Goethe

Bronze, life-size, 1930. Collection of Dr. M. Ćurčin, Zagreb. This is the best known of several studies of the great German poet which Meštrović has made over the years. Its reproduction was published in a number of Yugoslav periodicals, notably a special issue of *Nova Evropa* devoted to Goethe (May 1932) and as the frontispiece to the poet's translation of the Croat Moslem ballad *Hasanaginica*.

62. Monument of Gratitude to France

Bronze, 16 ft. high; total figure and base 35 ft., 1930. Kalemegdan Park, Belgrade. Erected in 1930 through the combined efforts of the Society of Friends of France and the Society of Former Students in France as a tribute to the wartime assistance of France to Yugoslavia. Two reliefs on the sides of the pedestal depict the Sorbonne as a symbol of France's contribution to the youth of Yugoslavia and on the other the collaboration of French and Yugoslav soldiers on the Salonika front.

63. *Monument to Simon Bolivar*
Plaster model, over life-size, 1930. Meštrović Museum, Zagreb.

64. *Petar Berislavić*
White, marble, 12 ft. by 16 ft., relief, 1933. Trogir, near Split, Dalmatia. This is a monument to the famous Croatian Bishop, a native of Trogir, who was killed fighting the Turks. It was set up in the loggia of the main square of Trogir in 1937, opposite the cathedral.

65. *John the Evangelist*
Bronze, over life-size, 1929. Meštrović Museum, Zagreb.

66. *The Evangelist Luke*
Bronze, over life-size, 1929. Meštrović Museum, Zagreb.

67. *Cyclops*
Bronze, study, 9 in. high, 1928. Meštrović Gallery, Split, Dalmatia.

68. *Head of Moses*
Marble, 4 ft. high, 1926. Bezalel Museum, Jerusalem. The artist's interest in Moses as a prophet and leader of men first appeared in England in 1915 when he did a number of studies, both busts and full-length figures. In 1930 he was commissioned to do a bronze *Moses* which was given to the Czechoslovakian President, Thomas Masaryk, by King Alexander of Yugoslavia. This monumental head was carved in 1926 and remained in his Zagreb home until 1950 when it was donated by the artist to the State of Israel on the anniversary of its independence.

69. *Cyclops*
Studies in plaster, 1928-29. Meštrović Gallery, Split, Dalmatia.

70. *Prophet*
Drawing, brown chalk, 1940. Meštrović Museum, Zagreb. One of a considerable number of drawings done during the artist's imprisonment in Zagreb in 1941.

71. *Prophet*
Drawing, brown chalk, 1940. Meštrović Museum, Zagreb.

72. *Women under the Cross*
Drawing, conte crayon, 1941. Meštrović Museum, Zagreb.

73. *Woman under the Cross*
Walnut relief, slightly under life-size, 1941. Collection of the artist, South Bend, Indiana.

74. *Gregory, Bishop of Nin*
Bronze, 26 ft. high, 1926. Split, Dalmatia. Monument to the tenth-century bishop who defended the right of the Croats to use old Slavonic (Glagolitic) in Roman Catholic Church services. This liturgy is still in use. The idea of such a monument was conceived during the First World War and, after considerable discussion with government officials, was accepted as Meštrović's gift to the town of Split. It stood originally in the peristyle of Diocletian's palace when it was unveiled November 29, 1929. During the Second World War it was removed by the Italian occupation forces, but later restored to a new position in front of the Golden Gate of Diocletian's palace. A smaller preliminary study for this figure was cast in bronze and presented by the sculptor to the city of Varaždin in 1931.

75. *Woman under the Cross*
Detail of walnut relief, life-size, 1941. Collection of the artist, South Bend, Indiana.

76. *Magdalene under the Cross*
Walnut relief, life-size, 1941. Collection of daughter, Marica Meštrović, South Bend, Indiana.

77. Noli me tangere
Drawing, conte crayon, 1941. Meštrović Museum, Zagreb.

78. St. Jerome
Oil on wood, 1945. Meštrović Gallery, Split, Dalmatia. A variant of the *St. Jerome* studies (see Fig. 85) with the familiar motifs of the Madonna and Child, Crucifixion and musical angels hovering as visions above him.

79. Pietà
Drawing, brown chalk, 1942. Collection of the University of Minnesota, Minneapolis.

80. Pietà
Drawing, conte crayon, 1941. Collection of the artist, South Bend, Indiana. A study for the later Pietà.

81. Christmas Song
Oil on wood, 1945. Collection of the artist, South Bend, Indiana.

82. Calvary
Oil on wood, 1945. Meštrović Gallery, Split, Dalmatia. A partial realization of several drawings of figure groups, particularly the women at the foot of the Cross and the Christ.

83. Last Supper
Oil on wood, 1945. Meštrović Gallery, Split, Dalmatia. Related to the relief later executed for Meštrović's chapel in Split.

84. The Argument of Job
Oil on wood, 1945. Collection of the artist, South Bend, Indiana. A development of the *Job* in the Syracuse University Collection (Fig. 87) into a curious disputation theme.

85. St. Jerome
Drawing, conte crayon on brown paper, 1945. Collection of Syracuse University, Syracuse, New York.

86. St. Jerome
Bronze, 4 ft. 6 in. high, 1954. Croatian Franciscan Fathers Home, Washington, D.C.

87. Job
Bronze, over life-size, 1945. Collection of Syracuse University, Syracuse, New York.

88. Author of the Apocalypse
Travertine, over life-size, 1946. St. Jerome Institute, Rome.

89. Pietà
Marble, one and one half times life-size, 1942-46. Collection of the artist; located in Sacred Heart Church, Notre Dame University, South Bend, Indiana. A massive five-and-one-half ton Carrara marble piece, this is probably the artist's most monumental accomplishment of the second war period. Begun in Rome in 1942, based on drawings made while in prison in Zagreb, it was finished in time for the large Metropolitan Museum exhibition in New York in 1947 and became one of its most dramatic attractions.

90. Pope Sixtus V
Travertine, over life-size, 1942. St. Jerome Institute, Rome.

91. St. Jerome
Travertine, over life-size, 1942. St. Jerome Institute, Rome.

92. Pope Pius XII
Bronze, life-size, 1942. St. Jerome Institute, Rome.

93. St. Francis of Assisi
Bronze, life-size, 1924. Banac Collection, Dubrovnik, Croatia. Owned by Božo Banac, prominent shipowner and son-in-law of the elder Račić for whom the Memorial Chapel in Cavtat was built in 1922.

94. St. Francis of Assisi Receiving the Stigmata

Plaster relief, over life-size, 1946. Church of San Francesco, Rome. The plaster model for the granite relief now in the principal Franciscan church of Rome was finished in Rome in 1946, shortly before the artist left for America.

95. Persephone

Onyx, life-size, 1945-46. Collection of Marta Srepel-Meštrović.

96. Supplicant Persephone

Bronze, over life-size, 1945-46. Collection of Syracuse University, Syracuse, New York. The tragic myth of Persephone, daughter of Zeus and Demeter who was abducted by Pluto to become queen of the nether regions, had a special appeal to Meštrović as a feminine parallel to his *Jerome-Job* series. As in the *Supplication,* it is not so much the personal experience that is expressed, as the identity with humanity's sufferings of the war and its unsolved problems. With characteristic consistency the theme is a development of earlier religious motifs, notably the *Mary Magdalene* (Fig. 31) as she appears with upstretched arms as a single figure and at the foot of the Cross in the Crucifixion scene. The *Supplicant Persephone* was purchased by popular subscription by the graduating class of 1955 as its gift to Syracuse University.

97. Supplication

Travertine, 1946. Collection of the artist, South Bend, Indiana. Significant as a new form of expression of a mood of prayerful appeal. Related to the *Jerome* and *Mother at Prayer,* or *Mother's Offering* (Figs. 86, 40, 41) ideas on the one hand and the *Mary Magdalene* and *Persephone* (Figs. 31, 96) on the other, its meaning seems less personal and more in general terms of humanity's hope of deliverance.

98. Atlantid

Bronze, life-size, 1946. Collection of the artist, South Bend, Indiana. The *Atlantid,* a form of nude caryatid whose burden is an inner spiritual struggle, is based more on the *Psyche* (Fig. 45) than the idea of the Kossovo caryatids. As such, it is again a significant parallel to the *Persephone, Jerome* and *Job* of the same period.

99. Croatian Rhapsody

Marble, life-size, 1947. Collection of Syracuse University, Syracuse, New York. A more compact and dramatic version of the earlier *Gusla Players* such as the 1929 *Girl with Guitar* (Fig. 55) and here specifically identified by the artist as expressing the folk aspirations of Croatia.

100. Prometheus

Plaster sketch, 26 in. high, 1946. Collection of the artist, South Bend, Indiana.

101. Portrait of Mrs. Meštrović

Plaster, life-size, 1947. Collection of the artist, South Bend, Indiana. A significant portrait not only because of its subject, whose distinguished appearance and gracious character have made the artist's home a center for innumerable devoted friends, but also because it expresses a quality of individual elegance and human dignity which is reflected in other works of this new period of development.

102. Cardinal Stepinac

Plaster study for the bronze bust (Fig. 103).

103. Cardinal Stepinac

Bronze, life-size, 1947. Archbishop Stepinac High School, White Plains, New York. Aloysius Cardinal Stepinac, Archbishop of Zagreb (1937) had long been a close friend of the artist and was famous for his outspoken opposition to Nazis and Fascists, as well as Communists, before his imprisonment by the Communist regime of Marshal Tito. This portrait was intended not so much as a representation of physical characteristics, but as a genuine character portrayal. It stresses those qualities of personal dignity, human sympathy and a saint-like courage that have made him almost an international symbol. As such it bears a remarkable similarity to the *Portrait of Mrs. Meštrović* done this same year (Fig. 101).

104. *Mother and Child*

Onyx, life-size, 1946. Syracuse Museum of Fine Arts, Syracuse, New York. One of the most genuinely joyful pieces in the artist's entire output. Of particular attraction is the soft glow and transparent tan color which the material lends to the total moving form.

105. *Isis and Horus*

African onyx, life-size, 1947. Collection of the artist, South Bend, Indiana. Isis, the Egyptian Goddess of Motherhood and Fertility with her son Horus, the Apollo-like God of Day, are presented as pagan parallels to the Christian Madonna and Child. Though the artist's Christian and Catholic faith is deep and sincere, it is equally liberal in its recognitions of universal values and reflects his dedication to humanitarian ideals regardless of race, creed or culture.

106. *Happy Youth*

Bronze, life-size, 1946. Collection of the artist, South Bend, Indiana. Executed in Rome, Italy, this figure of a youthful girl represents an innocent, happy Persephone before her ravishment by Pluto. It is a striding, not a posed figure. The face wears a curious enigmatic smile which has something archaic to it, that contradicts the expressive movement which the forceful twist of hip and torso lends to the total figure.

107. *Head of St. Christopher*

Plaster, over life-size, 1947. Collection of the artist, South Bend, Indiana.

108. *Mother and Child*

Plaster, over life-size, 1947. Collection of the artist, South Bend, Indiana.

109. *The Meštrović Home*

Split, Dalmatia, 1930-36. Now the Meštrović Gallery.

110. *Our Lady of the Angels: The Račić Memorial Church*

Marble, 45 ft. high, 1920-22. Cavtat, Dalmatia. General view of the exterior.

111. *Račić Memorial Church*

Interior: view of the high altar.

112. *Račić Memorial Church*

Interior: detail, Angel with Soul.

113. *Račić Memorial Church*

Interior: high altar with altar of St. Roch.

114. *Pietà*

Bronze, over life-size, 1932. St. Mark's Church, Zagreb.

115. *Study of Archangels*

Drawing, conte crayon, 1938. Meštrović Gallery, Zagreb. Project for over life-size fresco decorations intended for the dome of the Meštrović Chapel in Otavice, Dalmatia.

116. *The Memorial Church of Our Lady*

Biskupija, Dalmatia, 1932-38. The Memorial Church of Our Lady in Biskupija, a small village near Knin, was begun in 1932 in memory of the pious Croatian King Zvonimir, who reigned in the eleventh century and is revered for his goodness and humility. Built with indigenous granite, the style is reminiscent of the early medieval Croatian churches which have a strikingly modern character. A seated figure of *Christ the Shepherd* was set in the wall over the entrance while a *Madonna and Child* with several other pieces decorated the interior. These were almost completely demolished during the Second World War.

117. Bronze Doors

Meštrović Family Chapel of the Holy Redeemer, 1934, Otavice, Dalmatia. Represented are portrait reliefs of the artist's parents, himself and other members of his immediate family.

118. Mourning over Christ

Limestone, life-size, 1934. Chapel of the Holy Redeemer, Otavice, Dalmatia.

119. After Birth

Bronze, life-size, 1934. This is a bronze version of which the limestone original is in the Chapel of the Holy Redeemer, Otavice, Dalmatia. Bronze versions of *After Birth* and *Mourning over Christ* are in the Meštrović Gallery, Split, Dalmatia.

120. Crucifixion

Bronze, under life-size, 1933. St. Mark's Church, Zagreb. Above a side altar.

121. St. Mark's Church

Zagreb. Interior, showing choir with *Crucifix, Pietà* and *Madonna* in place.

122. Christ on the Cross

Bronze, 15 ft. high, 1933. St. Mark's Church, Zagreb. The series of figures for St. Mark's was begun in 1932 at the request of the artist's friend and fellow patriot Monsignor Svetozar Ritig, the parish priest of the church.

123. St. Mark, the Evangelist

Granite, over life-size, 1932. St. Mark's Church, Zagreb.

124. Christ in the Tomb

Marble altar frontal, life-size, 1932. St. Mark's Church, Zagreb.

125. The Meštrović Chapel of the Holy Cross

Split, Dalmatia, 1937-39. View of interior. In 1937-39 Meštrović built a small chapel on the grounds a short distance from his home in Split. Situated on a peninsula overlooking the Adriatic Sea, it had originally been the site of a twelfth-century church and cloister. Much of the old stone and wall remains were used in the reconstruction and contributed to the timeless and solid indigenous character of its architecture. The essential purpose of the artist was to provide a suitable setting for the *Life and Passion of Christ* which he had begun to carve in relief during the First World War. After the vicissitudes of war, imprisonment, exile and emigration to the United States, he completed the series in 1954 and presented the shrine-like ensemble as his gift to the Croatian people.

126. Crucifix

Wood, over life-size, 1917. The Meštrović Chapel, Split, Dalmatia.

127. The Happy Angels (The Nativity)

Walnut relief, 3 ft. 10 in. by 2 ft. 8½ in., 1917. Meštrović Gallery, Split, Dalmatia.

128. The Nativity (Madonna and Angels)

Walnut relief, 4 ft. by 6 ft., 1917. Meštrović Chapel, Split, Dalmatia.

129. Flight into Egypt

Walnut relief, 4 ft. 10 in. by 6 ft., 1938. Meštrović Chapel, Split, Dalmatia.

130. *Christ among the Doctors*
Walnut relief, 5 ft. 8 in. by 6 ft., 1940.
Meštrović Chapel, Split, Dalmatia.

131. *The Sermon on the Mount*
Walnut relief, 6 ft. 4½ in. by 6 ft., 1940.
Meštrović Chapel, Split, Dalmatia.

132. *Christ and the Woman
of Samaria*
Walnut relief, 3 ft. 10½ in. by 6 ft.,
1927. Meštrović Chapel, Split, Dalmatia.

133. *Raising of Lazarus*
Walnut, 1940. Meštrović Chapel, Split,
Dalmatia. Destroyed by fire during Second World War and replaced by the
1943 version (Fig. 134).

134. *Raising of Lazarus*
Walnut relief, 7 ft. 4½ in. by 6 ft.,
1943. Meštrović Chapel, Split, Dalmatia.

135. *The Temptation*
Walnut relief, 6 ft. by 3 ft. 3 in., 1917.
Meštrović Chapel, Split, Dalmatia.

136. *Christ and Mary Magdalene*
Walnut relief, 4 ft. 10 in. by 6 ft., 1939.
Meštrović Chapel, Split, Dalmatia.

137. *Christ in Gethsemane*
Walnut relief, 4 ft. 2½ in. by 6 ft., 1940.
Meštrović Chapel, Split, Dalmatia.

138. *Christ Driving the Money
Changers from the Temple*
Walnut relief, 6 ft. by 3 ft. 3 in., 1917.
Meštrović Chapel, Split, Dalmatia.

139. *The Deposition*
Walnut relief, 5 ft. 10 in. by 6 ft., 1917.
Meštrović Chapel, Split, Dalmatia.

140. *Christ in Gethsemane*
Walnut relief, 4 ft. by 6 ft., 1917. Col-
lection of Mrs. Kosor, Dubrovnik,
Dalmatia.

141. *He Is Risen*
Walnut relief, 4½ ft. by 6 ft., 1943.
Meštrović Chapel, Split, Dalmatia.

142. *Noli me tangere*
Walnut relief, 4 ft. by 6 ft., 1943. Meštrović Chapel, Split, Dalmatia.

143. *The Sad Angels*
(Lamentation over Christ)
Walnut relief, 5 ft. 8 in. by 4 ft. 3 in.,
1917. Meštrović Gallery, Split, Dalmatia.

144. *The Ascension*
Walnut relief, 6 ft. by 2½ ft., 1953.
Meštrović Chapel, Split, Dalmatia.

145. *Tomb of the Unknown
Soldier*
Granite, 50 ft. high, 1935-38. Avala,
near Belgrade. The tomb was commissioned by King Alexander and designed
as a massive sarcophagus raised on a
base of five four-foot plinths. Its two
entrances, from the east and west, symbolize the dual orientation of the Yugoslav people, while the four granite caryatids at each entrance are peasant women
clothed in characteristic regional cos-
tumes to represent the various provinces
of the country.

146. *Tomb of the Unknown
Soldier*
Detail of western entrance.

147. *Mila Gojsalić*
Plaster, over life-size, 1957. Poljica, near
Split, Dalmatia. The monumental figure
of *Mila Gojsalić*, the seventeenth-century peasant girl famous in the Croatian
folk songs for her heroic opposition to
the Turkish invaders, was given to the
people of Poljica as testimony to peasant
will for freedom and independence.

148. *John the Baptist*
Plaster, over life-size, 1954. Baptistry, Split, Dalmatia. This is a photograph of the plaster model sent to Yugoslavia, again as the artist's gift to his native people. The ancient Baptistry in Split, which was once a Roman temple of Bacchus, was constructed by Emperor Diocletian and later turned into a Christian chapel.

149. *Andrija Kačić Miošić*
Bronze, life-size, 1957. Franciscan Monastery at Zaostrog, Croatia. Monument to the Franciscan priest whose epic poems had been set to music and sung as popular folk songs accompanied by the *gusle*.

150. *The Njegoš Monument*
Drawing for the tomb of Petar Njegoš, 1932-1958. The idea of a mausoleum to honor the great Montenegrin poet, Petar Petrović Njegoš (1813-51) and Prince Bishop, as a national shrine, originated with King Alexander in 1932. The monument was to be erected on the peak of the high and massive Mt. Lovčen. A squared sarcophagus form similar to the *Tomb of the Unknown Soldier* is guarded by falcons on each corner and two pairs of ram-headed sphinxes at the entrance. After King Alexander's murder in Marseilles, the project was abandoned. But after the Second World War the people and government of Montenegro asked the artist to undertake the project again, which he agreed to do as his gift to the Montenegrin people. The grey-granite figure of the poet is over three times life-size, and is placed in a large and monumental rectangular chamber with an oval ceiling.

151. *The Njegoš Monument*
Plaster sketch, 1932. Meštrović Museum, Zagreb.

152. *The Njegoš Monument*
Granite, 1958.

153. *The Njegoš Monument*
Detail.

154. *The Njegoš Monument*
Detail.

155. *The Njegoš Monument*
Detail.

156. *Icarus*
Walnut, under life-size, 1947. Collection of the artist, South Bend, Indiana. Icarus was the son of Daedalus, the builder of the Cretan labyrinth in which both father and son were later imprisoned. They escaped by means of wings made of feathers. Icarus flew too close to the sun, so that the wax of his wings melted and he plunged to his death in the sea. The idea of flight and liberation had interested the artist, but has in most cases been used in the Christian religious sense as in the *Ascension* (see Fig. 144) rather than the pagan mythological. *The Fall of Icarus* has not been developed beyond this preliminary study.

157. *The Fall of Icarus*
Plaster, 12 in. high, 1954. Collection of the artist, South Bend, Indiana.

158. *Weeping Women*
Marble, 4 ft. high, 1956. Collection of the artist, South Bend, Indiana.

159. *Study of an Archer*
Drawing, red chalk, 1952. Collection of the artist, South Bend, Indiana. One of several preliminary studies for Odysseus killing the suitors of Penelope. Notice the difference in concept between the angular distortion and rhythmical expression noted in the 1917 studies for the *Archers of Domagoj* (Fig. 35) and the more plastically contained and individual three-dimensional form here.

63

160. *The Archers of Domagoj*
Grey marble relief, 4 ft. high, 1955. Collection of the artist, South Bend, Indiana.

161. *Girls with Musical Instruments*
Mahogany, 6 ft. by 3½ ft., 1956. Collection of the artist, South Bend, Indiana.

162. *Visitation*
Walnut relief, life-size, 1957. Collection of the artist, South Bend, Indiana.

163. *Joseph the Carpenter*
Plaster, 18 in. high, 1957. Collection of the artist, South Bend, Indiana.

164. *Madonna and Child*
Mahogany, life-size, 1957. Sacred Heart Church, Winnetka, Illinois.

165. *Joseph the Carpenter*
Walnut, life-size, 1957. Sacred Heart Church, Winnetka, Illinois.

166. *Migrating Peoples*
Clay study for the Jewish Memorial, life-size, 1952.

167. *Contemplation*
Walnut, life-size, 1952. Collection of the artist, South Bend, Indiana.

168. *The Guslar*
Walnut, life-size, 1954. Collection of the artist, South Bend, Indiana. A full length console-like figure of the traveling ballad singer with his *gusle* slung over his shoulder.

169. *Portrait of President Everett N. Case*
Bronze, over life-size, 1954. Collection of Colgate University, Hamilton, New York.

170. *Portrait of Chancellor William P. Tolley*
Bronze, over life-size, 1954. Collection of Syracuse University, Syracuse, New York. Meštrović has always maintained a warm and lasting affection for his many friends the world over. This is especially true of Dr. Tolley, Chancellor of Syracuse University, who appointed him Professor and sculptor-in-residence at Syracuse University and invited him to make his home in this country after the trying circumstances of the Second World War.

171. *Portrait of I. A. O'Shaughnessy*
Bronze, life-size, 1956. Collection of Notre Dame University, South Bend, Indiana. Well-known Chicago philanthropist whose generosity made possible both the new O'Shaughnessy Hall and sculptor's studio at Notre Dame University.

172. *Portrait of F. C. Morgan*
Bronze, life-size, 1957. The Montreal Museum of Fine Arts, Montreal, Quebec.

173. *Pope Pius XII*
Bronze, over life-size, 1957. Memorial Library of Pope Pius XII, St. Louis, Missouri.

174. *Jewish Memorial*
Preliminary study in plaster, 1952. This was one of several studies for a gigantic memorial to the six million Jews who lost their lives through Nazi oppression. It was intended for Riverside Drive in New York City, but has never been carried out. Another scheme which has been carried through to the full-scale working model involves a towering figure of Moses pointing to the Tablets of the Law toward which are moving a group of people massed in the form of a phalanx.

175. *Prophet*
Plaster, 15 in. high, 1956. Collection of the artist, South Bend, Indiana.

176. *Study for Moses*

Plaster, 15 in. high, 1953. Collection of the artist, South Bend, Indiana. One of several studies for the Jewish Memorial. One of these was given to the Temple Society of Concord in Syracuse by the artist.

177. *Blind Homer*

Plaster, 15 in. high, 1956. Collection of the artist, South Bend, Indiana. A small preliminary sketch for Fig. 179; one of several variations of this famous classical theme which parallels his own *Guslar* subjects.

178. *Prophet Jeremiah*

Limestone, life-size, 1952. Collection of the artist, South Bend, Indiana. Though Meštrović's basic approach to sculpture has always been in terms of the human figure, there are many and varied examples in which the medium and the shape of the material have dictated the final form. This studiously writing *Prophet* is one of the best examples in which the total design has followed the original block, even to the stylized treatment of shoulders, hair and crisp features of the face.

179. *Blind Homer*

Plaster, life-size, 1956. Collection of the artist, South Bend, Indiana.

180. *Head of Blind Homer*

Plaster, over life-size, 1956. Collection of the artist, South Bend, Indiana.

181. *Feeding the Sick*

Marble relief, 1953. Bellevue School of Nursing, New York. One of six relief panels depicting various scenes from the activities of nursing.

182. *Socrates and His Disciples*

Bronze, 18 in. high, 1953. Collection of Syracuse University, Syracuse, New York. One of several preliminary studies for a proposed monument to the classical philosopher and teacher for the Syracuse University campus but never carried out.

183. *St. Antony*

Bronze, life-size, 1953. St. Antony's College, Oxford, England.

184. *St. Jerome*

Bronze, life-size, 1955. Croatian Church of St. Jerome, Detroit.

185. *St. Antony*

Plaster, 8 ft. high, 1954. Church of St. Antony, Belgrade. The statue was sent to the Church of St. Antony in Belgrade as the artist's gift.

186. *St. Christopher*

Plaster, over life-size, 1955. Collection of the artist, South Bend, Indiana.

187. *The Prodigal Son*

Plaster, 2 ft. 3 in. high, 1954. Collection of the artist, South Bend, Indiana.

188. *Christ and the Children*

Plaster, 2 ft. 3 in. high, 1954. Collection of the artist, South Bend, Indiana.

189. *Head of St. John the Baptist*

Bronze, over life-size, 1957. Collection of the artist, South Bend, Indiana.

190. *St. Andrew*

Plaster, over life-size, 1957. Model for the bronze figure to be placed in front of the Episcopal Church of St. Andrew in Honolulu, Hawaii.

191. *Jacob's Well*

Bronze, over life-size, 1957. Collection of Notre Dame University, South Bend, Indiana. A development of the same theme used in the Meštrović Chapel series at Split. The base and well are of black marble. The monument is located in the center of a cloister-like patio connecting O'Shaughnessy Hall with the sculptor's studio on the university campus.

192. Man and Freedom
Bronze, 24 ft. high, 1953. Rochester, Minnesota. Placed against the north facade of the Diagnostic Building of the Mayo Clinic, this figure has been the subject of considerable discussion, since on first glance it would appear dwarfed by the expanse of the wall. The contrast in scale, however, is deliberate, whereby the seemingly unlimited area of luminous, textured space provided by the marble wall enhances the effectiveness of the figure and the ascension-like concept which it embodies. The Mayo Clinic project, where many of the country's best sculptors participated in the decoration of a strictly modern building, is one of the most striking examples of successful collaboration between contemporary architects and sculptors. The Meštrović figure particularly demonstrates both the success and further possibilities of a three-dimensional figure composition within the strict limitations of a contemporary architectural design.

193. Man and Freedom
Total view of the north facade of the Diagnostic Building of the Mayo Clinic. Ellerbe and Company, architects; Warren T. Mossman, art consultant.

194. Crucifixion
Limestone relief, 8 ft. by 22 ft., 1956. Trinity Lutheran Church, Rochester, Minnesota.

195. Crucifixion
Detail. Fig. 194.

196. Crucifixion
Mahogany, over life-size, 1957. Notre Dame University Chapel, South Bend, Indiana.

197. Crucifixion
Detail. Fig. 196.

198. Father Lopez Memorial
Bronze, 11 ft. high, on green granite base, 1958. Mission of Nombre de Dios, St. Augustine, Florida. A monument to Father Francisco Lopez de Mendoza Grajales, the missionary priest who accompanied the Spanish crew of Don Pedro Menendes de Aviles as they landed at St. Augustine to establish the Mission of Nombre de Dios on September 8, 1565. It was here that Father Lopez offered the first parish Mass in what is now the United States. The gesture carries the expression of praise to the Lord and the invocation of His blessing on this land of the future. This monument and the Pietà (Fig. 200) were commissioned by Archbishop Joseph Hurley.

199. Mary the Immaculate Queen of the Universe
Limestone relief, 17 ft. 9 in. high, 1957. National Shrine of the Immaculate Conception, Washington, D.C.

200. Pietà
Bronze, over life-size, 1958. Near Mercy Hospital and Immaculata High School, Miami, Florida. This recent example of the familiar Pietà theme was conceived as a memorial to modern martyrs, whose portraits are carved in relief in the circular granite wall which forms the backdrop of the Pietà group. These constitute the heroic churchmen who have opposed Communist oppression the world over. They include Cardinal Mindszenty of Hungary, Cardinal Stepinac of Yugoslavia, Stefan Cardinal Wyszynski of Poland, Archbishop Joseph Beran of Czechoslovakia, Bishop Francis X. Ford, Brooklyn missionary who was murdered by the Chinese Communists, and Bishop Patrick J. Byrne, apostolic delegate in Korea, who was imprisoned by the North Koreans and died in prison.

66

Illustrations

1. *At the Well of Life*

2. *At the Well of Life*

3. *At the Source of Life*

4. *Tolstoi*

5. *The Kossovo Temple*

6. *Marko Kraljević*

7. *Marko Kraljević*

8. *Banović Strahinja*

9. Srdja Zlopogledja

10. *The Maiden of Kossovo*

11. *Widows*

13. *Memories*

14. *Widow*

17. *Caryatids and Sphinx*

Widow with Child

18. *Caryatid*

19. *Vase with Frieze of Dancers*

20. *Vase with Frieze of Warriors*   21. *Vase with Frieze of Warriors and Peasants*

22. *My Mother*

23. *My Father*

24. *Portrait of the Artist's Mo*

25. *Portrait of Auguste Rodin*

27. Portrait of Lady Ratcliffe

Archangel Gabriel

29. *Madonna and Child*

31. *Mary Magdalene under the Cross*

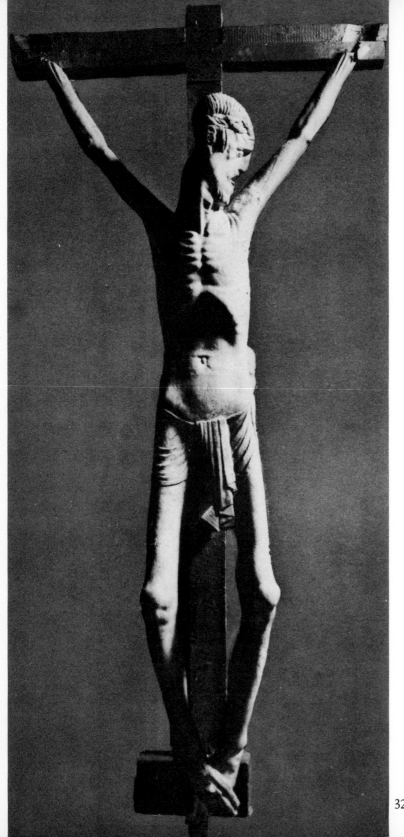

32. *Christ on the C*

33. *Moses*

34. *Moses*

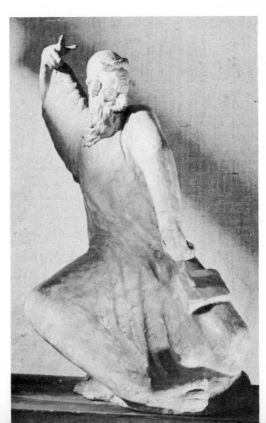

35. *The Archers of Domagoj*

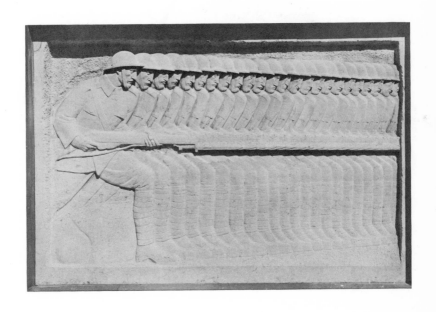

36. *The Canadian Phalanx 1914-1918*

37. *Portrait of the Artist's Wife and Child*

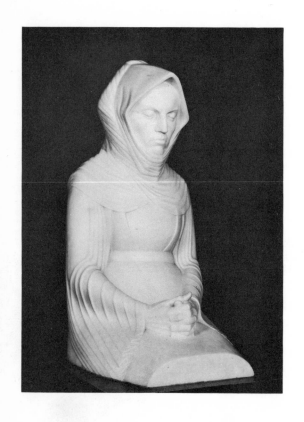

39. *My Mother*   40. *My Mother at Pr*

41. *Mother's Offering*

42. *Woman by the*

44. *Dreaming*

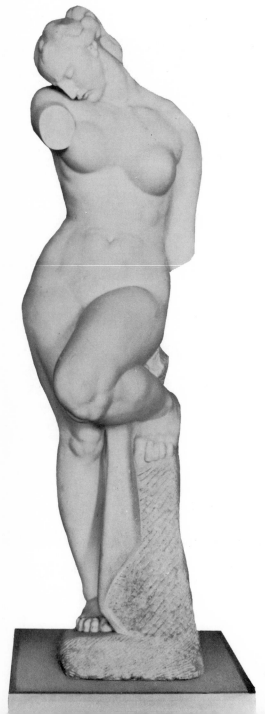

45. *Psyche*

46. *Woman with a Harp*

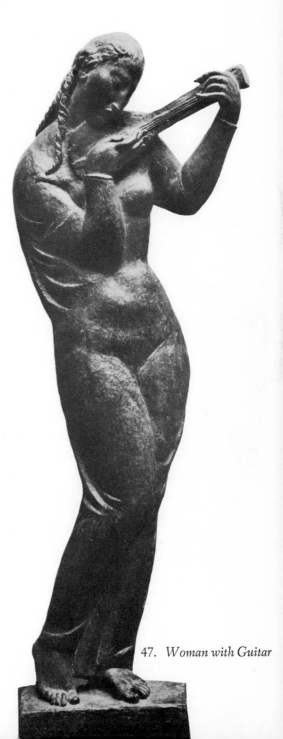

47. *Woman with Guitar*

48. *Madonna and Child*

51. *Console Figure*   52. *Console Figure*

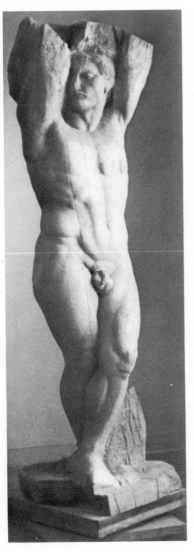 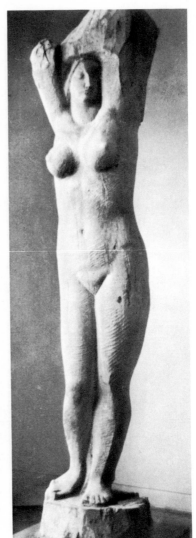

53. *Adam*   54. *Eve*

55. *Girl with Guitar*

56. *Marko Marulić*   57. *Marko Ma*

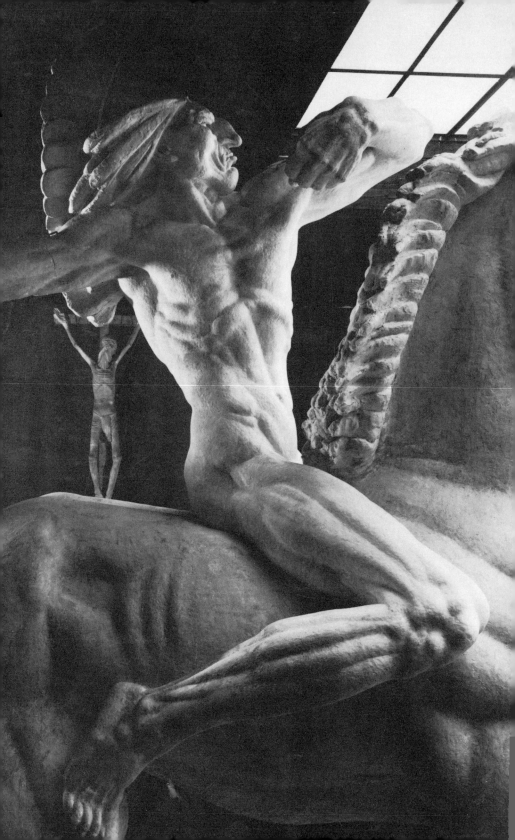

60. *Indian with Spear*

61. *Goethe*

62. *Monument of Gratitude to F*

63. *Monument to Simon Bolivar*

64. *Petar Berislavić*

66. *The Evangelist Luke*

John the Evangelist

67. *Cyclops*

68. *Head of Moses*

69. *Cyclops*

70. *Prophet*

71. *Prophet*

72. *Women under the Cross*

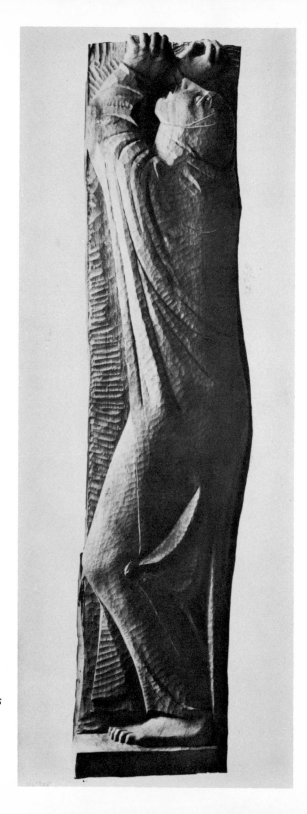

73. *Woman under the Cross*

75. *Woman under the Cross*

76. *Magdalene under the Cross*

77. *Noli me tangere*

78. *St. Jerome*

79. *Pietà*

80. *Pietà*

81. *Christmas Song*

82. *Calvary*

83. *Last Supper*

85. *St. Jerome*

86. *St.* J

ST. JEROME THE PRIEST
A.D. 341 — 420
GREATEST DOCTOR OF THE CHURCH

I. MESTROVIC

87. *Job*

88. *Author of the Apocalypse*

90. *Pope Sixtus V*

Pietà

91. *St. Jerome*

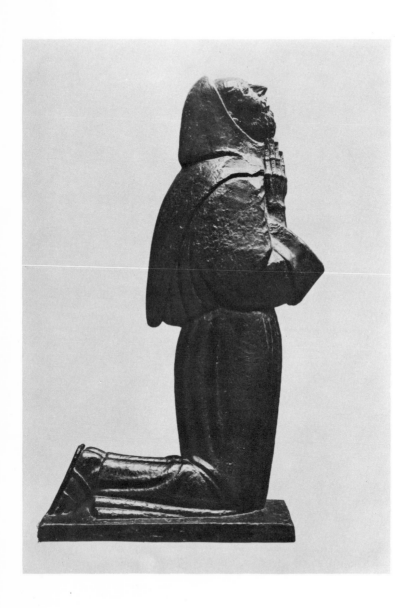

93. *St. Francis of Assisi*

94. *St. Francis of Assisi Receiving the Stigmata*

95. *Persephone*

96. *Supplicant Persepho*

PERSEPHONE
BY
IVAN MESTROVIC

97. *Supplication*

98. *Atlantid*

99. *Croatian Rhapsody*

00. *Prometheus*

101. *Portrait of Mrs. Meštrović*

102. *Cardinal Stepinac*

103. *Cardinal Stepinac*

104. *Mother a*
Child

105. *Isis and Horus*

106. *Happy Youth*

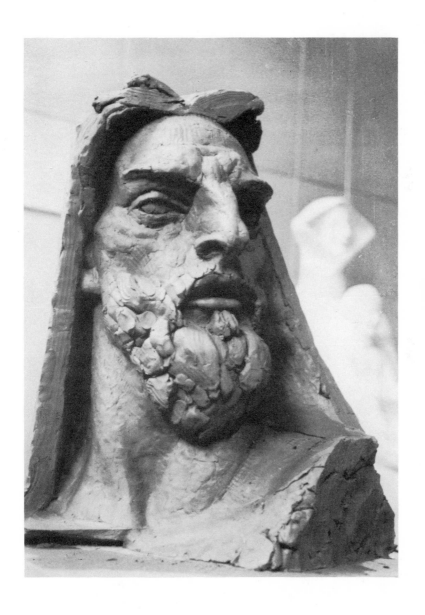

107. *Head of St. Christopher*

108. *Mother and Child*

109. *The Meštrović Home*

110. *Our Lady of the Angels: The Račić Memorial Church*

111. *Račić Memorial Church*

112. *Račić Memorial Church*

113. *Račić Memorial Church*

114. *Pietà*

116. *The Memorial Church of Our Lady*

117. *Bronze Doo*

118. *Mourning over Christ*

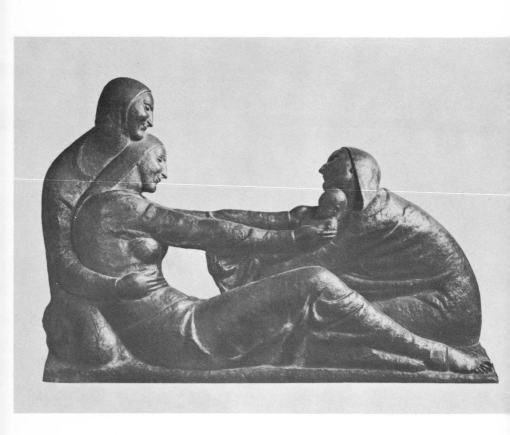

119. *After Birth*

120. *Crucifix*

121. *St. Mark's Church*

122. *Christ on the Cross*

123. *St. Mark, the Evangelist*

124. *Christ in the Tomb*

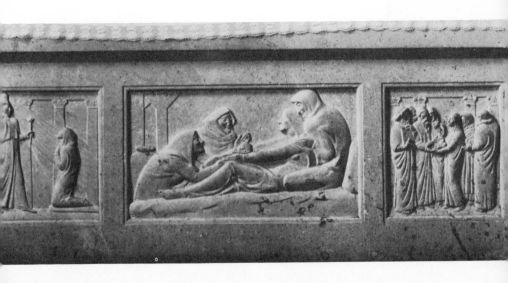

125. *The Meštrović Chapel of the Holy Cross*

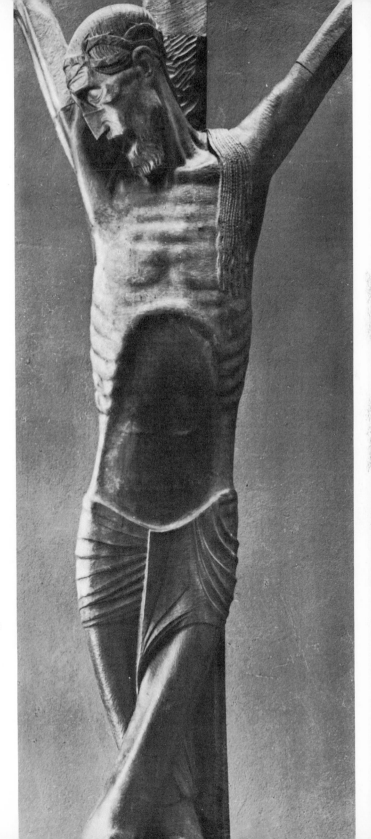

126. *Crucifix*

127. *The Happy Angels* (The Nativity)

128. *The Nativity* (Madonna and Angels)

129. *Flight into Egypt*

130.   *Christ among the Doctors*

131. *The Sermon on the Mount*

132. *Christ and the Woman of Samaria*

133. *Raising of Lazarus*

134. *Raising of Lazarus*

135. *The Temptation*

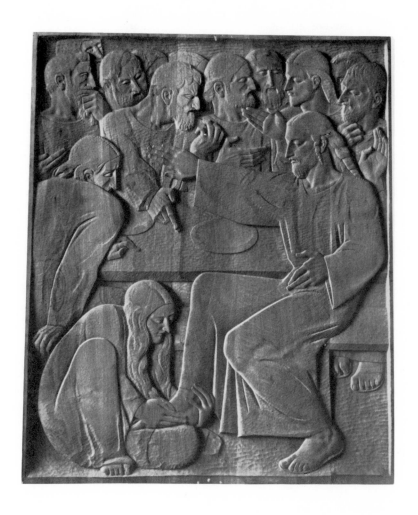

136. *Christ and Mary Magdalene*

137. *Christ in Gethsemane*

138. *Christ Driving the Money Changers from the Temple*

139. *The Deposition*

141. *He Is Risen*

143. *The Sad Angels* (Lamentation over Christ)

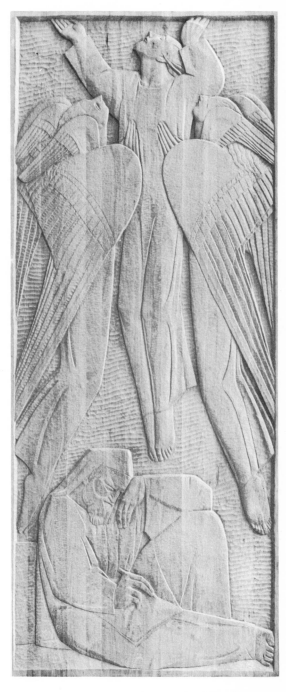

144. *The Ascension*

145. *Tomb of the Unknown Soldier*

146. *Tomb of the Unknown Sold*

147. *Mila Gojsalić*

148. *John the Baptist*

149. *Andrija Kačić Miošić*

153. *The Njegoš Monument*

155. *The Njegoš Monument*

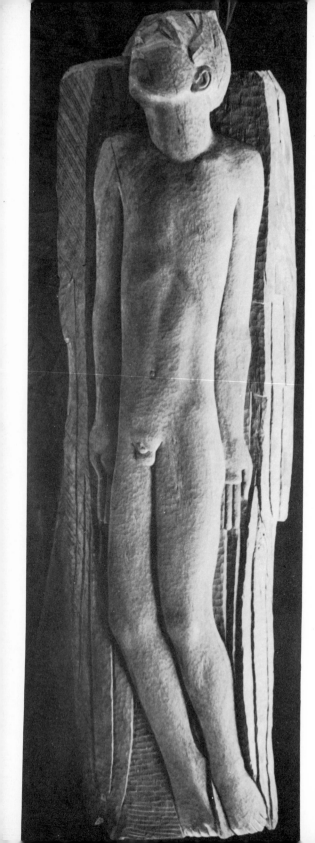

156. *Icarus*

157. *The Fall of Icar*

158. *Weeping Women*

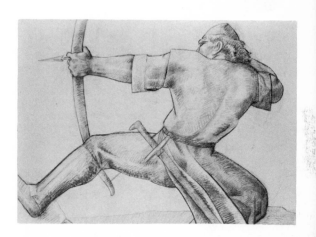

160. *The Archers of Domagoj*

161. *Girls with Musical Instruments*

162. *Visitation*

163. *Joseph the Carpenter*

164. *Madonna and Child*   165. *Joseph the Carpenter*

166. *Migrating Peoples*

167. *Contemplation*   168. *The Guslar*

169. *Portrait of President Everett N. Case*

170. *Portrait of Chancellor William P. Tolley*

171. *Portrait of I. A. O'Shaughnessy*

172. *Portrait of F. C. Morgan*

173. *Pope Pius XII*

174. *Jewish Memorial*

175. *Prophet*

176. *Study for Mo*

178. *Prophet Jeremiah*

Blind Homer

179. *Blind Homer*

181. *Feeding the Sick*

182. *Socrates and His Disciples*

183. *St. Antony*

185. *St. Antony*

186. *St. Christopher*

187. The Prodigal

188. *Christ and the Children*

Head of St. John the Baptist

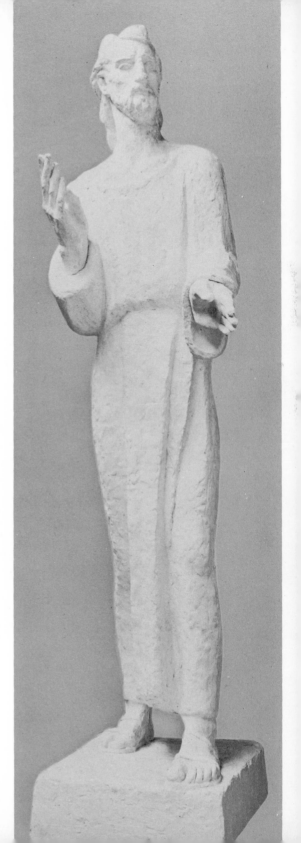

190. *St. Andrew*

191. *Jacob's Well*

192. *Man and Freedom*

193. *Man and Freedom*

194. *Crucifixion*

195. *Crucifixion*

197. *Crucifixion*

199. *Mary the Immaculate Queen*
of the Universe

200. *Pietà*